OECD Studies on Water

Reforming Economic Instruments for Water Resources Management in Kyrgyzstan

OECD

BETTER POLICIES FOR BETTER LIVES

This work is published under the responsibility of the Secretary-General of the OECD. The opinions expressed and arguments employed herein do not necessarily reflect the official views of OECD member countries.

This document and any map included herein are without prejudice to the status of or sovereignty over any territory, to the delimitation of international frontiers and boundaries and to the name of any territory, city or area.

Please cite this publication as:
OECD (2016), *Reforming Economic Instruments for Water Resources Management in Kyrgyzstan*, OECD Studies on Water, OECD Publishing, Paris.
http://dx.doi.org/10.1787/9789264249363-en

ISBN 978-92-64-24935-6 (print)
ISBN 978-92-64-24936-3 (PDF)

Series: OECD Studies on Water
ISSN 2224-5073 (print)
ISSN 2224-5081 (online)

The statistical data for Israel are supplied by and under the responsibility of the relevant Israeli authorities. The use of such data by the OECD is without prejudice to the status of the Golan Heights, East Jerusalem and Israeli settlements in the West Bank under the terms of international law.

Photo credits: Cover © iStock.com / Arkady Chubykin

Corrigenda to OECD publications may be found on line at: *www.oecd.org/about/publishing/corrigenda.htm*.

Acknowledgements and disclaimers

This project was undertaken by the OECD with the financial support of the European Union and the governments of Norway and Switzerland. Their contribution is gratefully acknowledged.

The project was implemented through the ongoing National Policy Dialogue (NPD) on water conducted in Kyrgyzstan in co-operation with the European Union Water Initiative (EUWI).

ACTeon was commissioned for analytical work. The main authors of the report are Pedro Andrés, Garzón Delvaux and Gloria De Paoli (ACTeon). Local water and environment specialists – Kalyibek Zhunusbaev, Taisia Neronova and Anarkul Choitonbeava – also contributed to this report and the implementation of the project. Alexandre Martoussevitch at the OECD provided essential oversight and inputs into the project and this report.

The authors are grateful for the co-operation, comments and data provided by government and nongovernment local stakeholders and also by international partners. Finally, the authors are very grateful to Aziza Djienbekova (Bishkek, Kyrgyzstan) for her translation services throughout the project; to Krzysztof Michalak and Xavier Leflaive (OECD) for their useful comments, to Shukhrat Ziyaviddinov (OECD EAP Task Force Secretariat) for formatting this publication and to Meleesa Naughton and Mark Foss (external consultants to the OECD EAP Task Force) for commenting on and copy-editing the report.

Disclaimers

Financial data on revenues generated by specific economic instruments were presented by respective Kyrgyz institutions upon an official request from the Department of Water Management and Melioration at the Ministry of Agriculture and Melioration of the Kyrgyz Republic, or following direct request by the project team. The consultant does not bear any responsibility for the accuracy of these data, or eventual inconsistencies with data provided by the same institutions to other parties.

Table of contents

Figures

Tables

Boxes

Abbreviations and acronyms

AP	Action Plan
DWM&M	Department of Water Management and Melioration, Ministry of Agriculture and Melioration
EC	European Commission
EECCA	Eastern Europe, the Caucasus and Central Asia (*region*)
HH	Households
KGS	Kyrgyz som
KR	Kyrgyz Republic
lcd	litres per capita per day
NPD	National Policy Dialogue
NRW	Non-Revenue Water
NSC	National Statistical Committee
O&M	Operation and Maintenance
Oblast	Administrative territorial unit (above rayon)
OECD	Organisation for Economic Co-operation and Development
POP	Persistent Organic Pollutant
PP	Polluter Pays Principle
n.a.	not applicable
NFEP	National Fund for Environment Protection
NCS	National Statistical Committee of the Kyrgyz Republic
Rayon	Administrative territorial unit (below *oblast*)
SAEPF	State Agency for Environmental Protection and Forestry under the Government of the Kyrgyz Republic
UNECE	United Nations Economic Commission for Europe
USD	United States Dollar
VGP	Viability Gap Funding
Vodokanal	Municipal Water Utility in Urban Areas
WBI	Water-Borne Infections
WRM	Water Resources Management
WSS	Water Supply and Sanitation

Exchange rates as of 4 May 2014: EUR 1 = KGS 75; USD 1 = KGS 55 (KGS 48.5 in 2011).

Executive summary

As part of the ongoing National Policy Dialogue (NPD) on water policy conducted in co-operation with the EU Water Initiative (EUWI), Kyrgyzstan has committed to enhance the use of economic instruments for water resources management to improve the management of surface and groundwater resources, including the quality of the resource. The reform would be very timely as by strengthening incentives for improving water use efficiency economic instruments could help to better balance growing demand for water (not least due to demand from export-led agriculture and tourism as key drivers of economic growth in Kyrgyzstan) with the available fresh water resources (the annual run-off will likely drop after 2050 due to negative impact of climate change) thus ensuring greater levels of security of water supply (presently, many farmers experience water shortages over the vegetation period). Also the reform could help to make the water sector more financially autonomous and less dependent on state support.

This report builds upon, and complements, the previous work on this topic in Kyrgyzstan (OECD, 2013); it presents recommendations on introducing or reforming the following economic instruments for water resources management identified as priorities with stakeholders through the NPD:

- surface water abstraction charges (including non-consumptive uses)
- environmental pollution fees
- tariffs for irrigation water
- specific land-tax rates for the Issyk-Kul Biosphere reserve
- tariffs for urban water supply and sanitation
- product tax (including import duty) on selected products that contribute significantly to diffuse water pollution in Kyrgyzstan.

For each instrument, various reform scenarios and implementation options are identified and assessed following the *Impact Assessment Guidelines* (European Commission, 2009). Specifically, for each economic instrument in question, the potential impacts of each reform option (scenario) were assessed in terms of **environmental, economic and fiscal, and social impact** (see section 2 on methodology for detail). Where data needed for the assessment were lacking, the authors sought **experts**.

The methodology contrasts the potential revenue and cost recovery prospects of each economic instrument, compared to the budget required to meet Kyrgyzstan's water management objectives; the financial, socio-economic and environmental implications of reform are analysed for each option. Actions corresponding to the recommended reform scenarios are presented in the form of a draft Action plan (**AP**).

Main findings

1. The implementation of recommendations will *(i)* help mobilise substantial additional financial resources for water resource management, through fiscal revenue and tariffs, *(ii)* contribute to a greater degree of financial sustainability for Kyrgyz water utilities (Vodokanals*)* and *(iii)* reduce the state irrigation system's dependence on public subsidies for the operation and maintenance (O&M) of water networks.

2. The introduction of **surface water abstraction charges** for both consumptive and non-consumptive uses (initially for big industries and hydropower stations only) will not only help generate significant additional public revenues annually (from KGS 390 million to KGS 2.5 billion per annum), but also create incentives for improving water use efficiency.

3. The proposed **reform of environmental pollution fees** will help reduce water pollution from point sources. Pollutants that most contribute to diffuse (non-point source) pollution of water resources in Kyrgyzstan include pesticides, mineral fertilisers and machinery lubricants with mineral oil. Introduction of a product tax and equivalent custom duty levied on selected products – particularly on agricultural chemicals (such as pesticides) with rates dependent on toxicity class and on lubricants – will help significantly reduce diffuse water pollution in Kyrgyzstan. Additional public revenues generated by this instrument (estimated at KGS 50-85 million per annum) could strengthen more cost-effective forms of state support to agriculture and the water sector (e.g. more efficient irrigation techniques and better rural infrastructure, including rural water supply and sanitation [WSS]).

4. The introduction of **new land-tax rates** in the Lake Issyk-Kul area – increased and better differentiated – would help capture a proportion of the rent related to the high environmental and recreational value of land in the Issyk-Kul Biosphere reserve. Eventually, increased land tax revenues (estimated at KGS 164 million per annum) could be used to improve water resource management and for other local environmental and social priorities.

5. The financial sustainability of water services – irrigation as well as water supply and sanitation services – is addressed primarily through the restructuring of water tariffs (the introduction of two-part tariffs with fixed and variable volumetric components), as well as an increase in tariff rates.

These ambitious water management objectives can be progressively developed and implemented through **appropriate sequencing** of reforms outlined by the AP for each economic instrument. A well-thought **staged approach** to reforms will also help mitigate or reduce eventual political resistance to the proposed options.

The proposed reforms will generally not have any significant negative impact on the economy (e.g. on businesses, consumers and households, innovation and research and specific regions and sectors). At the same time, **a gradual and well-sequenced implementation** will bring positive environmental, fiscal and social benefits. Overall, the reforms will help align water management policy to the broader development objectives of Kyrgyzstan such as the development of tourism and export-led agriculture in determining water demand. In addition, reduced reliance on public subsidies for O&M of water services will free up significant public funds; these can then be used for capital investment in rehabilitation and extension of water infrastructure and for strengthening the existing social support system through targeting vulnerable socio-economic groups.

Chapter 1

Overview and water management objectives of Kyrgyzstan

This chapter briefly presents the main objectives of the study and the list of economic instruments it focuses on.

Following the request of the governments of Kyrgyzstan and of Armenia, the OECD has embarked on an initiative to support further reform of economic instruments for water management in both countries. This initiative was launched in co-operation with the EU Water Initiative in the context of the National Policy Dialogues (NPD) on water ongoing in the two countries, and encompasses the following broad objectives:

- **Clarify the key objectives** of water management to be pursued by the proposed reforms in both countries.
- **Develop** a **set of options** for the design and level of economic instruments in question.
- **Assess** the proposed options, in terms of expected environmental and socio-economic impacts.
- **Identify the prerequisites for reform**, highlighting the required and/or desirable changes to the enabling environment (e.g. to regulatory and institutional frameworks, governance…) needed for reform.

In Kyrgyzstan, based on previous projects that identified and assessed key instruments for water resources management (see OECD, 2013, 2011a), as well as debates in the NPD context, research focused on the following economic instruments:

- user charges for urban water supply and sanitation
- tariffs for irrigation water
- environmental pollution charges
- surface water abstraction charges (including non-consumptive uses) for large industrial water users
- specific land-tax rates for Issyk-Kul Biosphere reserve (see Box 1.1)
- product tax (including import duty) on selected products (i.e. pesticides and lubricants) contributing significantly to diffuse water pollution, complemented by a deposit-refund system.

Box 1.1. **Changes in the management of the Biosphere Territory of Issyk-Kul**

Until recently, a vehicle entry fee into the Biosphere Territory of Issyk-Kul provided some revenue for environmental protection. The present initiative planned to propose reforms to the fee system to improve its management.

In May 2013, however, the fee system was scrapped. The State Agency for Environmental Protection and Forestry (SAEPF) is considering potential replacements, but no decisions have been made. Following exchanges with SAEPF, this report decided to explore the implications of specific land-tax rates **in the Biosphere Territory of Issyk-Kul** to contribute to environmental and water management objectives.

Source: Interviews with the State Agency for Environment and Forestry (SAEPF) representatives.

Based on the results of the assessment (OECD, 2013), this report outlines and assesses various reform options for the economic instruments noted above, using the *Impact Assessment Guidelines* (European Commission, 2009). It addresses the following components of each instrument:

- issues related to the implementation of the economics instruments currently in place
- objectives and priorities of the proposed reform
- short description of the proposed scenarios for reform (for each instrument, two to three reform scenarios are proposed)
- impact assessment of the proposed scenarios.

The report presents recommendations in the form of a draft Action Plan.

References

OECD (2013), *Improving the Use of Economic Instruments for Water Resource Management in Kyrgyzstan: the Case of Lake Issyk-Kul Basin*, EAP Task Force, OECD Publishing, Paris, www.oecd.org/environment/outreach/Kyrgyzstan_Eis%20for%20WRM_2nd%20edition_ENG%20web.pdf.

OECD (2011a), *Strengthening financial planning and management for WSS in central government, municipalities and utilities of EECCA countries*, presentation on the national policy dialogue on financing strategy for urban and rural water supply and sanitation in the Kyrgyz Republic, Kiev, 24 April 2009, www.oecd.org/environment/outreach/42756430.pdf.

Chapter 2

Methodology for assessing reform options in Kyrgyzstan

This chapter briefly presents the main guiding principles applied in this study as well as the methodology for assessing individual economic instruments and reform options (scenarios for reform) and for presenting the results of the assessment.

For each reform option (scenario) expected environmental, social, economic and fiscal impacts are assessed and a synthesis of its policy implications is presented, while recommendations are formulated in the form of a draft Action Plan.

Presentation of results

The results of assessment of different reform options (scenarios) are summarised for each proposed option to provide a synthesis of its policy implications (see respective chapters and Annex C). To avoid complex and excessive information, this report does not include all of its original sources, data and calculations, but only key findings and figures (e.g. on revenue flows, affordability issues, etc.) supporting our assessment. Additional information and figures, as well as references to the original sources, can be found in the annexes.

Advanced versions of the report were discussed during two NPD meetings (on 18/10/2013 and 20/03/2014) and at an expert meeting (on 18/03/2014) in Bishkek – see Annex B.

Approach

The methodology of the assessment follows four complementary phases:

- Briefly review existing instruments and assess their performance based on the methodology recommended by the OECD (OECD, 2013).
- Define possible options (or scenarios) for the instruments selected for reform or introduction.
- Assess the economic, social and environmental implications for each option (or scenario).
- Identify the prerequisites to the enabling environment needed for each option proposed.

Figure 2.1 illustrates the steps followed in developing the study.

Figure 2.1. **Methodology of the study**

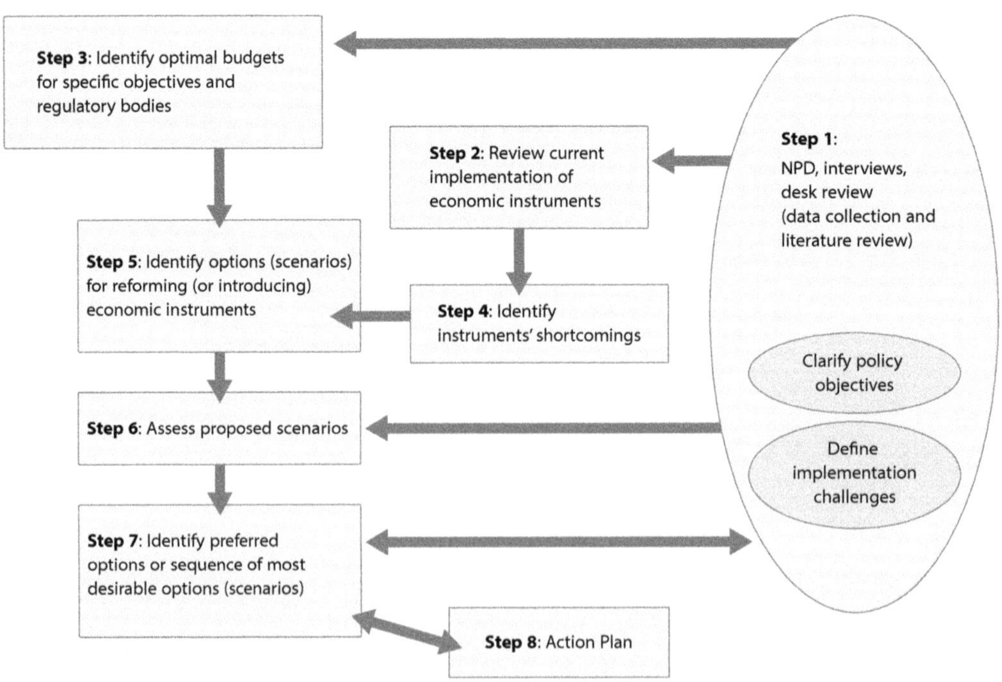

Source: Based on authors' own work.

Possible reform options are defined after a review of existing instruments and careful evaluation of their performance and shortcomings. The report pays particular attention to revenue-generating capacity of each instrument, in view of the overall policy objective of cost recovery. To guide development of these instruments (i.e. their scope and applicable fees), budget needs are mapped and assessed for different levels of water resources management (WRM). On the one hand, the methodology aims to contrast the revenue-generating prospects of each instrument and its respective development options. On the other, it identifies optimal budget needs, according to management objectives.

The options (scenarios) present three levels of possible development, mainly in terms of revenue generating capacity. In addition to revenue, however, the economic instruments are also expected to create incentives to reduce water pollution and improve water-use efficiency.

The first scenario showcases only a modest improvement compared to the current situation. The second scenario provides both clear incentives for higher standards of water management and sufficient resources for financing optimal management activities (operation and maintenance, capital investments, monitoring and research). These are complemented by a "middle of the road" scenario. This third scenario may be more feasible in the medium term, but may not provide enough funds for management activities. In addition, it may offer less powerful incentives for higher standards of water management.

The incentives are based on a key assumption: greater respect for the "polluter pays" and the "beneficiary pays" principles creates stronger incentives to reduce pollution and use water resources more efficiently, respectively.

The impacts' assessment aims to be comprehensive and to provide a balanced picture of the implications of reforming existing instruments or introducing new ones. The impact assessment framework is based on: European Commission (2009), *Impact Assessment Guidelines* 15 January 2009, SEC(2009)92. In turn, the proposed data requirement and indicators were identified to address specific information needs of this initiative. However, the exercise can neither be expected to provide information detailed enough to assess each option in full, nor to assess all impacts using factual data. Therefore, **expert judgments** were sought to complete the picture when data (quantitative or qualitative) were missing or not processed.

For each economic instrument in question, the potential impacts of each reform option (scenario) are assessed in terms of:

- The expected **environmental impact** – does the option have positive or negative environmental impacts? Special attention is paid to water, but air quality, soils, etc. are also investigated if and where relevant.
- The expected **economic and fiscal impacts** (including revenue generation for the public sector or for service providers) on economic activities – for example, is the viability of certain companies potentially at stake, and under which conditions?
- The expected **social impact**: is the option expected to impact on specific social groups? The issue of affordability is at the heart of this question.

Whenever possible and relevant, differences are made between direct and indirect impacts, and between short- and long-term impacts.

The options were developed and assessed based on a series of data and approaches combining quantitative and qualitative sources, as well as a thorough literature review, interviews and comments gathered during discussions at NPD meetings and other water-policy related events.

In practical terms, the following principles guide the main **priorities** for reform:

- Charge all user groups in a **fair and balanced way**, applying charge rates that are close to the actual environmental and resource cost of abstracted water.
- Introduce and gradually apply the **"beneficiary pays" and "polluter pays" principles.**
- Start by improving the performance of **existing instruments** (e.g. collection rates).
- **Engage with sectors with a low water cost to total cost ratio** when introducing new instruments, then address other sectors with higher water costs to total costs ratio.
- Harness an important **source of revenue** for water management: the fee (user charge, tax) revenues should cover operation and maintenance costs, and eventually cover future investments or even account for resource costs.
- Introduce a **more direct link between revenue from water-related instruments and water management expenditure**, compared to the current system governing natural resource use and environmental pollution fees.
- Support the improvement of **monitoring and metering systems,** as recommended in the recent OECD report (OECD, 2013).
- Ensure **policy coherence** among water management instruments, as well as with sectorial policies and international agreements.
- Focus on **medium-term** (5-7 years) scenarios as an interim step towards more ambitious long-term options. The timeframe chosen is in line with that of the National Sustainable Development Strategy for 2013-17.

All the recommended reforms outlined in the Action Plan include **supporting and accompanying measures** appropriate for the three main groups of water users: domestic users, farmers and industrial users.

Sources of information

Assessments in this report are based on several sources of information, in particular:

1. outputs and outcomes of previous projects in Kyrgyzstan (see OECD, 2013, 2011a)
2. additional data collection from national sources
3. interviews with government officials and water management specialists in charge of the management of the economic instruments proposed for reform (see list of officials interviewed in Annex A)
4. comments collected during and after the NPD, and expert meetings.

References

EC (2009), *Impact assessment guidelines*, 15 January 2009, SEC(2009)92, European Commission, Brussels.

OECD (2013), *Improving the Use of Economic Instruments for Water Resource Management in Kyrgyzstan: the Case of Lake Issyk-Kul Basin*, EAP Task Force, OECD Publishing, Paris, www.oecd.org/environment/outreach/Kyrgyzstan_Eis%20for%20WRM_2nd%20edition_ENG%20web.pdf.

OECD (2011a), *Strengthening financial planning and management for WSS in central government, municipalities and utilities of EECCA countries*, presentation on the national policy dialogue on financing strategy for urban and rural water supply and sanitation in the Kyrgyz Republic, Kiev, 24 April 2009, www.oecd.org/environment/outreach/42756430.pdf.

Chapter 3

Introducing surface water abstraction and water-body use charges in Kyrgyzstan

Three scenarios for reform of surface water abstraction and water-body use charges are assessed, and impacts of each scenario are synthesised in this chapter. Supporting and accompanying measures are proposed to facilitate implementation – these provide input to the draft Action Plan.

Rationale for reform

Surface water abstraction charges and water-body use charges (including non-consumptive uses) are economic instruments that **have not been mobilised to date** in Kyrgyzstan.

The total volume of surface water abstracted by different sectors in Kyrgyzstan (Table 3.1) – more than 8 billion cubic metres (m^3) per year – represents an important opportunity for developing charges for surface water abstraction. This resource is mainly allocated to agriculture for irrigation, a sector that accounts for 93% of total withdrawals of surface water; it is by far the most significant water-using sector of the economy. The estimated opportunity costs of using the water downstream are very high (Table 3.1), which calls for implementation of the "**beneficiary pays**" principle.

Table 3.1. **Surface-water withdrawal by sector in Kyrgyzstan and estimated opportunity costs**

Sector	Total annual withdrawal of surface water (million m^3)	Estimated opportunity costs of downstream water use (billion KGS per year)
Agriculture	7 447 (93%)	12.66
Industry	336 (4.2%)	0.57
Municipal water supply	224 (2.8%)	0.38
Total	**8 007**	**13.61**

Source: FAO, 2014.

The proposed reform in a nutshell

Abstraction and water-body use charges can be an important addition to the existing economic instruments for water management. Such charges are compatible with existing legal provisions in the 2005 Water Code of the Kyrgyz Republic. So far they have been an untapped source of revenue for water management and can become an important incentive for more efficient water use. A gradual reform of surface water abstraction charges could thus pursue the following **objectives**:

- **Short-term objective:** Introduction of surface water-abstraction charges for industries and water-use charges for hydropower and fisheries can reduce the burden on the central government's budget for water management. This could be linked to the application of permits for all users ("minimal" water management budget). **The proposed permit dimension could be in synergy with the currently reviewed permit system for environmental fees and its potential reform.**[1] Initially, it could be applied as a small charge for large industrial water users (which could more easily accommodate the charges) and water use for hydroelectricity generation (which would provide significant revenue). However, initial rates would be too low to provide either sufficient revenue for water management or strong incentives for more efficient water use.
- **Medium-term objective:** Increase of all charges related to sensitive water bodies (those for which the risk of resource depletion is high). Revenue from surface water abstraction charges must be sufficient to cover all recurrent expenses (operation and maintenance (O&M) and sector governance costs) involved in water management (the "optimal" water management budget has yet to be defined).

- **Long-term objective**: Water abstraction charges should cover all resource costs of water abstraction (including water for irrigation). They should provide a strong incentive for more efficient use of water resources, including reduced abstraction in agreement with the need to protect aquatic ecosystems (not estimated).

Based on these considerations, three gradual reform scenarios were developed.

Proposed scenarios: Description and expected impacts

The following two tables 3.2 and 3.3 provide for each scenario: *(i)* a synthesis of the scenarios; *(ii)* their expected impacts.

Table 3.2. **Proposed scenarios for reform of surface water abstraction charges**

Timeline	Current situation	Scenario I Introduction of abstraction charges (Short term)	Scenario IIb Partial implementation of abstraction charges (Medium term)	Scenario IIa Full introduction of abstraction charges, including irrigation (Long term)
Description and objective	Abstraction charges do not exist.	Surface water abstraction fees are introduced for the following sectors: • industry • WSS utilities • hydropower plants.	As per Scenario I. Covers a portion of the costs of water management, while accounting for potential affordability and political acceptability issues that might arise.	As per Scenario IIb, including water use for irrigation. The objective is to cover all expenditure related to water management (ideally, all O&M and sector governance costs).
Charge rates	n.a.	Introduction of a licensing/permitting system: Permits are issued for abstraction of surface water over a fixed volume threshold; the charge rate is set at KGS 0.1/m^3 for all uses.	Rates are set at KGS 1/m^3 for all consumptive uses. For non-consumptive water uses, the rate is set at 10% of the rate for consumptive water uses.	In this case the charge rates per m^3 are set at KGS 1 for consumptive uses and at KGS 0.5 for non-consumptive uses.
Applicability	n.a.	Application of all fees at permit level, i.e. water users should pay for the limit volume indicated in their permits = "*take or pay*" formula		
Revenue allocation	n.a.	All revenue goes to water management: e.g. 75% of all revenue returns to water management bodies, while 25% is allocated for research on water by the state; targeted social support to households and small farmers; and eventual support for innovations significantly improving water-use efficiency in industries and agriculture (e.g. drip irrigation).		
Coherence with existing legislation	Envisaged in the legislation (Water Code), but not yet implemented.			

Note: **n.a.**: not applicable.

Source: Author's own elaboration.

The revenue implications of the above scenarios are as follows:

Table 3.3. **Revenue implications for surface water abstraction charges reform**

Timeline	Current situation	Short-term, scenario I	Medium-term, scenario IIb	Long-term, scenario IIa
Expected additional revenue (in mln. KGS), per main water uses	**Revenue in 2011**		**Expected revenue**	
Industry and fisheries	0	50	500	500
Water utilities	0	22	220	220
Hydropower	0	290	290	1 450
Irrigation	0	0	0	7 447
Total	**0**	**372**	**1 010**	**9 617**

Source: Authors' own findings.

Expected impacts

In terms of impacts, each scenario brings similar, although gradually evolving results. The main difference is related to the possible introduction of irrigation networks as contributors to the surface water abstraction charges scheme under Scenario IIa, which is not considered in the other two scenarios.

Scenario I *(short term)*

The introduction of a surface water abstraction charge is expected to generate a marginal economic impact at general industry level: industrial organisations supplied with piped water by Vodokanals would pay in the range of KGS 5-10 per m^3. In turn, some indirect impact could be expected on water charges for households and, consequently, on potentially vulnerable social groups. Introducing surface water charges for non-consumptive uses by hydropower plants would increase the electricity tariff by around 5% from KGS 0.7-0.74 per kWh. This change, however, combined with a marginal increase in water bills, does not substantially impact the affordability of water supply or electricity services for households, including vulnerable social groups, if proposed accompanying measures are adopted during implementation.

Scenario IIb *(medium term)*

Higher surface water abstraction rate charges than in Scenario I should lead to innovation and increase of overall water efficiency levels. Most changes, however, are rather expected to come from higher energy prices and pollution control measures in industry. Similarly, households' electricity bills are expected to increase, on average, by up to 5%, which is considered manageable. Current affordability levels of water supply services are not expected to change. A very limited negative economic impact can be expected for fisheries and other industrial sectors.

Scenario IIa *(long term)*

This scenario includes abstraction charges for water use for irrigation networks and increasing non-consumptive water-use charges (e.g. for hydropower generation). The scenario clearly promotes innovation and increase of overall water efficiency levels by tackling the largest users of water. Since water use in industry is highly variable, water pricing is only expected to moderately influence water efficiency compared to other drivers such as energy prices and pollution control regulation. Earlier studies have shown: these various factors will push innovation towards new productive processes that involved higher water-use efficiency, among others (Egenhofer et al., 2012). Some limited negative economic impacts can be expected for hydropower production (if additional costs cannot be passed onto customers), fisheries and some industrial sectors (linked both to large volumes of water and electricity used). Electricity bills could increase by as much as some 20%, translating into a significant economic impact on household budgets and a critical need for supportive measures. Affordability levels of water supply services are not expected to change significantly; however, increased irrigation rates can have both direct and indirect impacts on rural households as food producers and water consumers.

Including surface water abstraction charges for irrigation under the proposed scenario increases equity among water users. At the same time, it raises affordability constraints, particularly for subsistence farmers. In turn, higher prices from irrigation water may also provide incentives for illegal borehole drilling. This possible adverse effect is expected to be limited by the cost of groundwater extraction, which currently combines higher drilling and pumping costs, and groundwater abstraction fees. The risk is, however, higher in areas with a low collection rate of groundwater abstraction fees.

For single users, water use is expected to decrease. However, the application of permits might entail a re-allocation of water use, and the total abstracted quantity in the future could increase beyond the allocation allowed by the present permits. This is, in essence, the Jevons' paradox (Polimeni et al., 2008): as water is made available, new uses (re-allocation) can be favoured, such as increasing irrigated land. Finally, improved water resources management is expected to generate positive environmental benefits.

Synthesis of impacts

Overall, the three scenarios are expected to have neutral or slightly positive economic and social impacts. With regards to environmental impacts, each of the three scenarios aims to enhance water management of surface water bodies in Kyrgyzstan; the positive result of the impact assessment is not surprising. In contrast, increasing water abstraction charges, especially for households, raises concerns about potentially negative social and economic impacts. The results of the impact assessment, however, highlight that such concerns may not necessarily materialise, or are limited in the medium term. The main economic impact for households and other stakeholders would come from water abstraction or water-use charges to be paid by hydropower plants since they will pass costs onto consumers. However, accompanying measures, such as strengthening of targeted social support to vulnerable households by fully compensating them for the additional expenses for electricity, can help mitigate potentially negative social impacts. This could be financed with a small fraction of the additional budget revenue generated under the proposed reform scenarios.

Under the long-term scenario, the delay in including irrigation networks as contributors to water abstraction charges allows for a gradual implementation of this new instrument.

The expected impacts of the proposed scenarios are summarised in Table 3.4.

Table 3.4. **Synthesis of expected impacts of water abstraction charges reforms**

	Impact compared to current situation	Scenario I	Scenario IIb	Scenario IIa
Economic and fiscal impacts	Businesses	0	0	0/-
	Innovation and research	+	+	+
	Consumers and households	0/-	0/-	-
	Public budget	+	++	++
	Water utilities and irrigation service providers	0/-	-	--
	Specific regions or sectors	0	0/+	0
	Overall impact	**+/0**	**+**	**+**
Social impacts	Vulnerable groups*	0	0	0/-
	Participation	0	0	0
	Public health and safety	0	0	0
	Overall impact	**+**	**0**	**0/-**
Environmental impacts	Climate	+/0	+	++
	Water quantity	+/0	+	+
	Water quality	+/0	+	+
	Water resources	+/0	+	+
	Overall impact	**+/0**	**+**	**++/+**

* Based on the assumption that eventual losses of vulnerable groups will be fully compensated from the strengthened social support system.

Source: Based on authors' own work.

Support and accompanying measures

In the wake of a possible introduction of surface water abstraction charges, a series of measures have been identified as prerequisites for its implementation and to enhance acceptability among relevant users.

In the medium term, the following five actions are highlighted as key to the enabling environment of the proposed reform:

- Prepare a draft regulation on surface water abstraction charges and submit it for approval to the government (the regulation should set rules, procedures and accountability for calculating and paying the charges, as well as establish sanctions for violations).
- Prepare and submit to Parliament a draft law on amendments to the Water Code and other water-related legislation (e.g. on WSS).
- Re-instate surface water use permits by amending existing legislation.
- Launch a diagnostic of industry needs for improving resource-use efficiency and pollution control (this should not be limited to water resources, but also to energy efficiency and other key resource inputs).
- Submit a proposal for a financing mechanism that would ensure that most new resources are earmarked for water management.

These measures are recommended for the draft Action Plan. In the long term, and in a spirit of gradual implementation:

- Prepare and submit to Parliament a draft law on amendments to the Water Code and other water-related legislation (foremost concerning the irrigation network).
- Provide a targeted support programme (including financing and guidance) for improvement of production processes to support innovation in resource intensity reduction (e.g. by introducing "*best available techniques*") and pollution abatement and control (better treatment).

Note

1. Environmental pollution fees are also assessed in this document (see following section).

References

Egenhofer, C., et al. (2012), *Which economic model for a water-efficient Europe?*, CEPS Task Force Report, 27 November 2012, Centre for European Policy Studies, Brussels.

FAO (2014), *FAOSTAT – FAO Statistics Division*, Food and Agriculture Organization, Rome, http://faostat3.fao.org/faostat-gateway/go/to/search/PESTICIDES/E.

Polimeni, J., et al. (2008), *The Jevons Paradox and the Myth of Resource Efficiency Improvements*, Earthscan, London.

Chapter 4

Reforming environmental pollution fees in Kyrgyzstan

Three scenarios for reform of pollution fees are assessed, and impacts of each scenario are synthesised in this chapter.

Rationale for reform

Water pollution fees are based on the "**polluter pays principle**" (PPP). They have been in place in Kyrgyzstan since the adoption of the 1999 Law on Environmental Protection.

Box 4.1. **Structure of the environmental pollution fees in KR**

The pollution fee for emitting any polluting substance is determined by a base rate per tonne of pollutant (KGS 1.2/tonne) multiplied by a coefficient reflecting the relative environmental risk of the substance (e.g. from KGS 0.01/tonne (for chlorides); up to KGS 21 120/tonne [for mercury] in 2009). Such rates apply within the limits specified in a pollution permit granted by the SAEPF (the permit system is under review; although the SAEPG grants permits, while the State Inspectorate for Technical Safeguards monitors the permits). Discharges detected beyond the maximum permitted limits are subject to charges at ten times the normative charge rate. The normative charge rate is furthermore multiplied by a coefficient for the ecological significance (varies from 1 to 3: for Lake Issyk-Kul, it is equal to 3) and ecological status (= 100 throughout the country) of the receiving water bodies and finally a coefficient for indexation of 2002 base values (reflecting the inflation accumulated since 2002).

Source: Adapted from OECD (2013), personal communication.

However, the actual performance of environmental pollution fees has been questioned. On the one hand, they do not cover the costs of environmental damage; on the other, they do not provide a real incentive for polluters to reduce their polluting discharges ("no dynamic efficiency").

Poor financial and technical resources to monitor the quality of wastewater and the application of pollution fees hinder implementation. The calculation of the pollution charges is complex. Since it is based on a very long list of pollutants, it is difficult to monitor actual discharges, calculate the total amount payable and enforce payments.

The revenue collected does not necessarily help fund water resources management. Instead, the revenue is allocated to Local Funds on Environmental Protection, which is used for general activities related to SAEPF's environmental mission; 25% are then transferred to the National Fund for Environment Protection (NFEP) and serve a variety of environmental objectives.

Finally, several key polluters are exempt from the fee, most prominently the Vodokanals, but also other utilities (e.g. district heating, energy providers, etc.).

The proposed reform in a nutshell

Environmental pollution fees constitute an important tool in the instruments available for water resources management in Kyrgyzstan. The proposed reform looks at how they could both generate more revenue and provide incentives for increased efficiency in water use and water conservation. A gradual reform of environmental pollution fees could thus pursue the following **objectives**:

- **Short-term objective:** Improve implementation of the current environmental pollution fee system by linking it to the application of permits[1] for all users and by *(i)* revising the calculation methodology, *(ii)* making pollutant-discharging industries pay the fees directly to the Republican Fund on Environment Protection; and *(iii)* making water utilities (Vodokanals) pay for discharges from households, the cost of which could be passed onto households by including it into WSS tariffs. Exemptions to the environmental pollution fees would remain for the general population and for public institutions. The allocation of financial resources would remain the same, i.e. with the Republican Fund on Environmental Protection.

- **Medium-term objective:** Remove all exemptions to the current environmental pollution fee system. The revenue collected through environmental pollution fees and other water management instruments (such as abstraction charges) would cover all recurrent expenses (O&M and sector governance costs) for adequate water management; the "optimal" water management budget would need to be defined. The allocation of financial resources would remain the same i.e. with the Republican Fund on Environmental Protection.
- **Long-term objective**: Increase environmental pollution fees to cover the costs of water pollution (including the resource costs) and to provide a clear incentive for pollution reduction measures, including for the protection of aquatic ecosystems and related uses (not yet estimated). The allocation of financial resources is exclusively dedicated to funding water management activities.

Based on these considerations, three reform scenarios were developed, as illustrated in Table 4.1.

Table 4.1. **Proposed scenarios for reform of environmental pollution fees**

Timeline	Current situation	Scenario I Review of current situation (Short term)	Scenario IIb Intermediate scenario (Medium term)	Scenario IIa Fuller application of the polluter pays principle (Long term)
Description and objective	Water pollution fees are based on the "polluter pays principle" (PPP). The fees are: *(1)* too low, so they do not recover the costs of enforcement; and *(2)* they do not provide a real incentive for polluters to change (i.e. no "dynamic efficiency"). Furthermore, water utilities are exempt from the current system.	The system of water pollution fees based on permits is maintained, but water utilities are no longer exempt. An indicative budget for cost recovery (O&M and capital) is included for reference, based on the 2003 proposal for reform of fee rates.*	It includes a modest increase of the base fee rate, and elimination of all exemptions (including water utilities). Covers part of the projected expenditure for water management, while accounting for affordability and political acceptability issues that might arise.	As per Scenario I, but revokes all exemptions. Covers a larger share of the costs related to water management (ideally, all O&M and sector governance costs).
Fee rates	Determined by the present base fee rate (KGS 1.2 per tonne of pollutant) multiplied by a coefficient reflecting the relative environmental risk of the polluting substance.**	Fees remain the same, but the calculation system is simplified.	The base rate is set at KGS 60 per tonne of pollutant (equivalent to 1/10th of the optimal budget calculated needs).	The base fee rate is increased to KGS 611.
Applicability	Rates apply within the limits specified in the pollution permit granted by the SAEPF. The permit system is under review.	Application of all fees as per the permits, i.e. water users should pay for the limit volume indicated in their permits = "*take or pay*" formula	Rates apply within limits specified in pollution permits granted by the SAEPF. The permit system is under review.	Not calculated based on permit, but rather on actual pollutant discharges.

*Assuming new base fee rate at KGS 280 per tonne of pollutant.

** In 2009, the rates varied between KGS 0.01/tonne (for chlorides) and up to KGS 21 120/tonne (for mercury) (+ special rates for Issyk-Kul multiplied by aforesaid coefficients).

Table 4.1. **Proposed scenarios for reform of environmental pollution fees** *(continued)*

Timeline	Current situation	Scenario I Review of current situation (Short term)	Scenario IIb Intermediate scenario (Medium term)	Scenario IIa Fuller application of the polluter pays principle (Long term)
Revenue allocation	Funds keep feeding both local and Republican Fund on Environmental Protection.	All revenue goes to water management and any social programme needed to take into account the potential effect of having the Vodokanals pay pollution fees. A proportion of funds could also be used for supporting innovation in water resource intensity reduction and water pollution abatement and control.	Funds keep feeding both local and Republican Fund on Environmental Protection.	
Coherence with existing legislation	Part of the current set of instruments of water management since the adoption of the 1999 Law on Environmental Protection.	Reforms are underway and the 2003 proposal relative to rates could be updated and submitted to Parliament.	Part of the current set of instruments of water management since the adoption of the 1999 Law on Environmental Protection.	

Source: Authors' own findings.

The budget and revenue implications of the developed scenarios are set out in Tables 4.2 and 4.3.

Table 4.2. **Budget implications of the developed scenarios**

"Optimal" water management budget (in mln. KGS)		
Function	**Budget in 2011**	**Optimal budget (estimate)**
Water protection measures	4.41	2 500
SAEPF on water quality	**4.16**	**2 500**

Source: Authors' own findings.

Table 4.3. **Revenue implications of the developed scenarios**

Timeline	Current situation	Scenario I (Short term)	Scenario IIb (Medium term)	Scenario IIa (Long term)
Sources of revenue	**Revenue (2011, mln KGS)**	**Expected revenue (mln. KGS)**		
Industry	3.21	4.2	252	1 961.74
Water utilities	0	0.8	40	444.19
Other polluters	0	0	?	?
Total	**3.21**	**5**	**392**	**2 500**

Source: Based on authors' own findings.

Expected impacts

In terms of impacts, each scenario brings similar, although gradually evolving results.

Scenario I is close to the current situation and reflects ongoing discussions within the Kyrgyz environmental sector. The single most important difference is the taxation of water utilities due to their untreated discharges. Following the current review of the application of fees at permit level, and taking into account the proposed simplification of the fees' calculation, average monitoring and reporting costs for businesses and for public administration would decline. Clearly, additional revenues will be generated, thanks to an improved collection rate from existing sources, and to the Vodokanals' contributions. Most of the changes would be expected in Bishkek and the Issyk-Kul Oblast as they would represent 45% and 28% of all current environmental fee revenue respectively. The general industry level would experience a marginal economic impact. Households could expect some economic impacts, consequently, vulnerable social groups could be affected. No significant changes in pollution levels and environmental conditions can be expected.

Scenario IIb (medium term) retains the same parameters as Scenario 1, but places greater emphasis on innovation and incentives to increase overall water treatment levels before discharge. Affordability levels of water supply services are not expected to change significantly (See Synthesis of impacts section). The resulting improvement in water management will have a very strong positive environmental impact. As in Scenario I, most of the changes can be expected in Bishkek and the Issyk-Kul Oblast. The amount of untreated discharges into water is expected to decrease.

Scenario IIa (long term) *inter alia* aims at increasing revenue from environmental pollution fees, and thus substantially contribute to pollution abatement efforts of environmental agencies and programmes. Scenario IIa has the same qualitative impacts as Scenario IIb, but in greater quantity, due to increased fees levied for pollutants.

Synthesis of impacts

Overall, the social and environmental impacts of the proposed reform would be positive. The most ambitious scenario is likely to have some negative financial impacts on industry and the Vodokanals, which are currently not subject to environmental pollution fees.

The three scenarios were designed to enhance water management of surface water bodies in Kyrgyzstan; the results of the preliminary impact assessment are in line with expectations. There are some important limitations to the exercise, however. Estimates of potential new revenue streams are not easily quantifiable. Consequently, they are prone to change as levels of discharges are expected to start falling with the increase of pollution fees.

The introduction of Vodokanals as a potential source of revenue for environmental pollution fees, and the transfer of additional costs onto customers raises the question of potential economic and social impacts for households. However, water bills are currently very low in Kyrgyzstan and accounted for 1.2% of the median household disposable income in 2009 (2011 data from the CIS Statistics Committee). More recent (2011 and 2012) data based on samples in several provincial towns show that, for the poorest quintile of households, water bills account for a larger share of disposable income, up to 5-6%. For wealthier households, water bills only represent about 0.2% to 0.7% of disposable income (see Annex D – Table D.7). The proposed changes, then, which would double or triple current fee rates, are likely to have an impact only on a fraction of the poorest quintile.

The expected impacts of the proposed scenarios are summarised in Table 4.4.

Table 4.4. **Reform of level and structure of environmental fees: Synthesis of the expected impacts of the reform scenarios**

	Impact compared to current situation	Scenario I	Scenario IIb	Scenario IIa
Economic and fiscal impacts	Businesses	0	0	0/-
	Innovation and research	+	+	+
	Consumers and households	0/-	0/-	-
	Public budget	+	++	++
	Water utilities and irrigation service providers	0/-	-	--
	Specific regions or sectors	0	0/+	0
	Overall impact	**+/0**	**+**	**+**
Social impacts	Vulnerable groups*	0	0	0/-
	Participation	0	0	0
	Public health and safety	0	0	0
	Overall impact	**+**	**0**	**0/-**
Environmental impacts	Climate	+/0	+	++
	Water quantity	+/0	+	+
	Water quality	+/0	+	+
	Water resources	+/0	+	+
	Overall impact	**+/0**	**+**	**++/+**

* Based on the assumption that eventual losses of vulnerable groups will be compensated from the strengthened social support system.

Source: Based on authors' own findings.

Support and accompanying measures

A series of measures have been identified to provide the enabling environment necessary for reform of environmental pollution fees (see Chapter 9 below).

Figure 4.1. **Proposed scenarios for the reform of water abstraction charges and environmental fees**

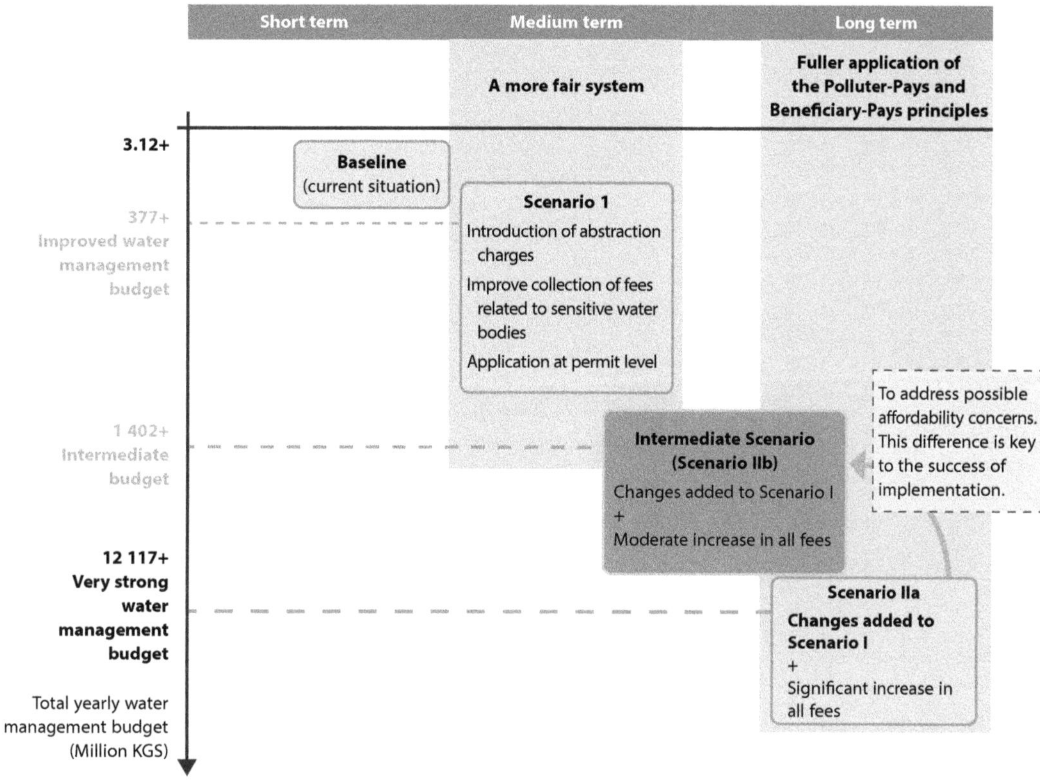

Source: Authors' own assessment.

Note

1. The permit system is under review and although the granting will continue to be managed by the SAEPF, the monitoring of the permits is to be handed to the State Inspectorate.

References

OECD (2013), *Improving the Use of Economic Instruments for Water Resource Management in Kyrgyzstan: the Case of Lake Issyk-Kul Basin*, EAP Task Force, OECD Publishing, Paris, www.oecd.org/environment/outreach/Kyrgyzstan_Eis%20for%20WRM_2nd%20edition_ENG%20web.pdf.

UNECE (2000), *Environmental Performance Review: Kyrgyzstan,* Environmental Performance Reviews Series No. 9, United Nations Economic Commission for Europe, New York and Geneva.

Chapter 5

Reforming irrigation tariffs in Kyrgyzstan

Five scenarios for reform of irrigation tariffs are assessed, and impacts of each scenario are synthesised in this chapter. Supporting and accompanying measures are proposed to facilitate implementation – these provide input to the draft Action Plan.

Rationale for reform

According to the state network, current tariffs for water used for irrigation in Kyrgyzstan peak at KGS 0.03 /m^3 during the growing season; in areas classified as having a severe (inhospitable) climate, tariffs are much lower at KGS 0.01/m^3. This tariff is for water supply from the state irrigation network to operators of on-farm irrigation networks (normally a water user association, or WUA); it forms only part of the final tariff charged to individual farmers. Based on this tariff, WUAs charge additional fees to cover the costs of administration and O&M of the irrigation network down to the farms. Thus, tariffs for water for irrigation vary between KGS 0.058 and 0.178/m^3 for end-users.

Box 5.1. **Cost structure and irrigation tariff**

Most costs of operating the state irrigation network are fixed (e.g. staff, maintenance of infrastructure, buildings), which remain the same irrespective of the volume of water supply. A simple volumetric tariff is applied, which only covers variable costs, thereby generating a deficit in the operation of the network. As such, a two-part tariff system would more adequately address the need to cover both fixed and variable costs of the state irrigation service.

Source: Various interviews and authors' own assessment.

In recent years, the tariffs paid by farmers for irrigation services only represent 10% of the funds required to cover O&M costs; the state effectively subsidises 90% of the financial costs through the state irrigation system. Evidence regarding the deterioration of irrigation services suggests the combined current funds from the state budget and user charges are insufficient.

The proportion of farmers' income spent on water for irrigation varies between 0.5% and 2.5%, which is low by international standards. There may be scope for an increase of the tariffs, while ensuring the service remains affordable.

A World Bank study found that farmers are prepared to pay between 5-30% of their income for irrigation services, depending on quality of the service (World Bank, personal communication). This suggests that most Kyrgyz farmers would pay more than they currently do. In addition, Aylward and other experts estimated the average economic value of water for irrigated agriculture in Kyrgyzstan at KGS 13/m^3 (ranging from KGS 0.46 to 92/m^3). On this basis, the current tariff of KGS 0.03 /m^3 represents an insignificant proportion of the economic value gained from water used for irrigation; there would be some potential for a tariff increase in line with the "beneficiary pays principle".

The proposed reform in a nutshell

The proposed reform of tariffs for irrigation would pursue the following objectives:

Short-term objective: Raise the financial revenue earmarked to strengthen the administrative capacity of water management agencies required for sustainable water management, proper administration of water resources, adequate monitoring and control, reporting, research and development.

Medium- to long-term objective: Significantly contribute to **full recovery of the costs** of irrigation services (including O&M costs, as well as partial and total capital costs, which are mainly understood as rehabilitation costs of existing infrastructure). Environmental and resource costs have not yet been estimated. Several reform scenarios were considered. In addition to a gradual increase in tariffs for water use for irrigation (hereafter referred to as "irrigation tariff"), a shift to a two-part tariff system (Box 5.2) was also explored.

Box 5.2. Introducing a two-part irrigation tariff

The first part of the irrigation tariff could be set to contribute to the fixed costs of providing irrigation services. It would be based on the area of irrigated land (per hectare) serviced by the irrigation network – even if farmers are not using that land. In practice, this would be charged in addition to land tax. The system of land tax collection is already well established in KR; it could be adapted to add the fixed cost of irrigation services to the appropriate tax rates for irrigated land in each oblast and rayon of Kyrgyzstan. This proposal would require the earmarking and transfer of this additional element of land tax to the Department of Water Management and Melioration, Ministry of Agriculture and Melioration (DWM&M) to cover the fixed costs of the irrigation network.

The second part of the irrigation tariff would cover the variable cost of providing irrigation services, such as the costs of electricity in areas where water is pumped. These costs vary according to the volume of water supplied to farmers; therefore, a variable charge (per m^3 of water) would be levied. The volumetric charge could also include an additional charge for the use of water as a natural resource (see above section on surface water-use charges); this would provide an incentive for efficiency of water use in irrigation and contribute to policy coherence between the two instruments.

Source: (OECD, 2013) and authors' own work.

Based on these considerations, reform scenarios were developed, as illustrated in Table 5.1.

Table 5.1. **Proposed scenarios for reform of tariffs for irrigation**

Timeline	Current situation	Short term: Scenario 0 Improvement of collection rates	Medium term: Scenario Ia Gradual increase in tariffs	Medium term: Scenario Ib Introduction of a two-part tariff for irrigation water	Medium to long term: Scenario IIb Removal of public subsidies for O&M	Long term: Scenario IIa Strong management possibilities
Description and objective	Revenue from irrigation tariffs represents around 10% of the funds required to cover the current O&M costs; i.e. public budget effectively subsidises some 90% of financial costs of providing service by the state irrigation system. Collection rates are estimated to be low, at some 50% of billing.	Tariffs remain the same, but the effectiveness of collection is increased from an estimated 50-95% of billing.	Reducing and eventually removing subsidies to irrigation service provision. The revenue collected would partially cover current O&M costs, but fall short of the optimal budget for managing the state irrigation system.	Introduction of a two-part tariff system. Covers most of the expenditure related to irrigation system management without state subsidies. The optimal budget for rehabilitation estimated at KGS 4 350/ ha/year.	Two-part tariff as in Scenario Ib. The objective of this scenario is to cover all O&M costs and partial rehabilitation (KGS 750/ha/yr) Increase of tariffs compared to Scenario Ib, but lower than in Scenario IIa.	Two-part tariff as in Scenario Ib. The objective of this scenario is to cover all O&M costs and partial rehabilitation (KGS 1 972/ha/yr) Increase of tariff rates compared to Scenario Ib.
Tariff rates	KGS 0.03/m³ during the growing season (can be lower at KGS 0.01/m³). Additionally, WUA charge for administration, O&M of irrigation network at on-farm level. Thus, irrigation services tariff for end-users vary between KGS 0.068 and 0.18/m³.	Tariffs remain the same.	Gradual increase of tariffs over a five-year horizon. Tariffs increase approximately by a factor of 10 from KGS 0.03 to 0.3/m³ i.e. a 60% increase per year for five years.	Introduces a "fixed costs" (FC) part (on average KGS 150/ha/year) for irrigated land area, and a "variable costs" (VC) (appr. KGS 0.05/m³ for water used + electricity cost for pumping and/or surface water abstraction charge (permits).	FC part (an average KGS 750/ha/year) for irrigated land area. VC (appr. KGS 0.2/m³) for actual volume of water used + electricity cost for pumping and/or surface water abstraction charge (permits).	FC part (an average KGS 1972/ha/year for irrigated land area.* VC (appr. KGS 0.5/m³) for actual volume of water used + electricity cost for pumping and/or surface water abstraction charge (permits).
Basis	Volume- and permit-based			Volume- and permit-based for the variable part of the tariff + land-tax based, according to the area irrigated for the fixed part of the tariff.		
Revenue allocation	All revenue goes to irrigation system management, and any associated social programme (DWM&M and WUA).					
Coherence with existing legislation	Part of the current set of instruments of water management, included in the Water Code.			The introduction of the two-part tariff requires an additional collection procedure to be added for the volumetric costs. Fixed costs can be linked to the existing land tax collection system, limiting the associated transaction costs.		

Note: **appr.** stands for "approximately".

Source: authors' own proposal and assessment.

Table 5.2. **Budget implications of proposed scenarios for reform**

	"Optimal" water management budget (in mln. KGS)	
Function	**Budget in 2010**	**Optimal budget**
Routine repairs	59.1	n.a.
Other operational costs	67.7	n.a.
Total budget of DWM&M	**681.6**	**1 064**

Note: **n.a.**: the figure is not available.

Source: Authors' own assessment based on DWM&M data.

Table 5.3. **Revenue implications of the proposed scenarios for reform**

Expected additional revenue (in mln. KGS)	**Current**	**Scenario 0**	**Scenario Ia**	**Scenario Ib**	**Scenario IIb**	**Scenario IIa**
Source	Revenue in 2010 (50% collection rate)	Potential revenue at 95% collection rate	Expected revenue under a 10-yr horizon	Expected revenue under a 10-yr horizon	Expected revenue under a 10-yr horizon	Expected revenue under a 10-yr horizon
Fixed charges	n.a.	n.a.	n.a.	**164**	**822**	**2 162**
Variable charges	n.a.	n.a.	n.a.	**206**	**824**	**2 060**
Tariff for irrigation	68.4	129	684	n.a.	n.a.	n.a.
Total	**68.4**	**Approx. 130**	**684**	**370**	**1 646**	**4 222**

Note: **n.a.**: not applicable.

Source: Authors' own findings.

Expected impacts

In terms of impacts, each scenario brings similar, although gradually evolving results.

Scenario 0

This scenario is a first step, ready to be implemented in the short term, in preparation for medium- and long-term reforms. It focuses on the efficiency of collecting current irrigation fees, with the same tariffs. As such, the scenario is expected to have impacts in terms of revenue for the operator of the state irrigation system (and hence for the public budget), but also some costs associated with billing and recovery of unpaid bills. Some impacts are expected on users that do not currently pay (i.e. free riders).

Scenario Ia

In addition to the progress in collection rate made under Scenario 0, Scenario Ia proposes changes that would involve low transaction costs for public administration; they could generate additional revenue by gradually increasing fees to cover the costs of O&M. The agricultural sector will be affected, although to a limited extent, under this scenario. Given the known willingness to pay for irrigation water, only marginal effects are expected in terms of affordability. Under the proposed tariffs for irrigation, no significant changes in volume of water use are expected.

Scenario Ib

Following Scenarios 0 and Ia, this scenario would constitute a crucial milestone for reform in the medium term by introducing a two-part tariff system. A more predictable revenue stream is expected to translate to a more reliable water supply across the irrigation system.

Irrigation water services are still expected to be affordable. However, current dependence on operational subsidies could be reduced, and more space could be offered for targeted social support if needed and relevant. This could lead to an increase in the promotion of innovation towards more efficient water use, especially if the state supports such projects.

Scenario IIb

This scenario constitutes the main objective to be pursued in the medium term. Under this scenario, revenue is expected to cover the costs of high levels of O&M, combined with incentives for innovation towards more efficient use of water. Due to increased financing, water management is enhanced and water supply becomes more reliable across the irrigation system.

At user (farmer) level, specific water consumption is expected to decrease. However, the total quantity of water used could increase beyond the present level due to Jevons' paradox: greater water use efficiency creates more water availability, which gives way to new uses for water, including a potential increase in the size of irrigated land.

Scenario IIa

Under this long-term scenario, previous measures are expected to be strengthened, and measures taken to promote innovation towards more efficient water and energy use. A steady revenue stream would ensure high levels of O&M and cover part of the capital costs of irrigation infrastructure.

The affordability of water irrigation services could be significantly affected; however, reduced dependence on operational subsidies would offer more room for targeted social support, if needed. A significant increase in water tariffs for irrigation could indirectly affect food prices for irrigation-dependant crops. Increased irrigation tariffs can have both direct and indirect impacts on rural households as food producers and water users. That said, the current share of water in total production costs is less than 1%, according to the National Federation of Water Users Associations; this provides significant room for tariff increase.

Water supply is more reliable across the irrigation system and is less vulnerable to the effects of climate change and climate variability.

As per Scenario IIb, water use per hectare or per tonne of produce is expected to decrease at user level. However, the total volume of water used could increase beyond present levels due, again, to Jevons' paradox.

The proposed sequence of reform implementation is presented in Figure 5.1.

Figure 5.1. **Proposed scenarios for the reform of irrigation tariffs**

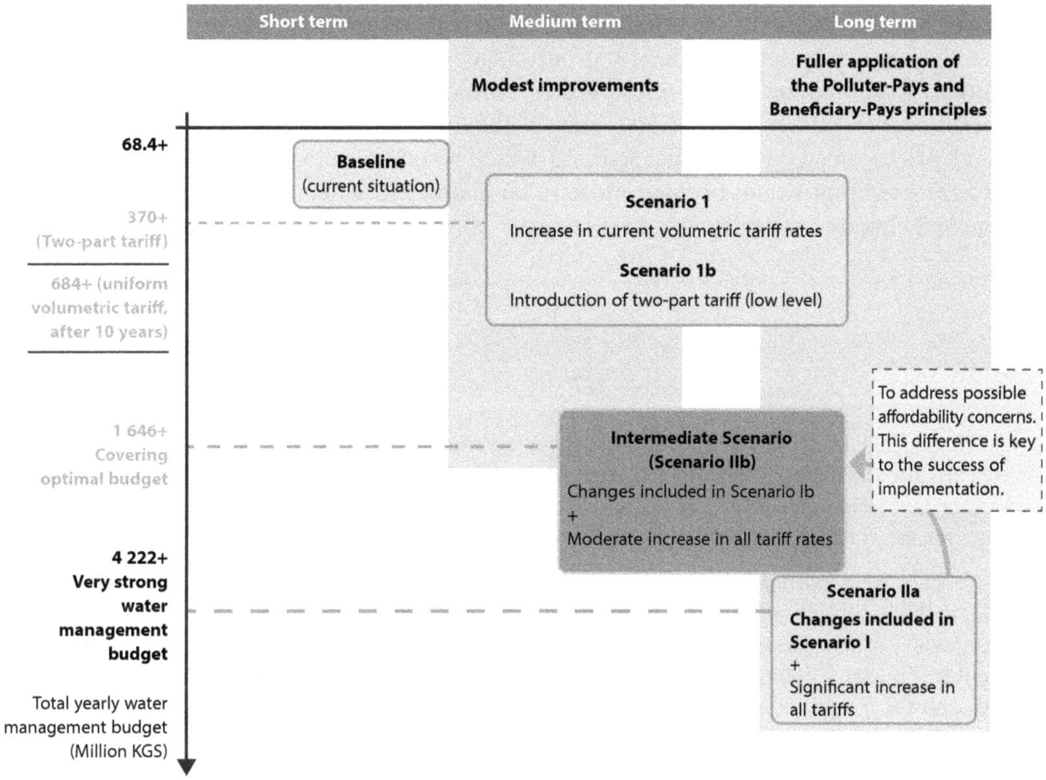

Source: Authors' own assessment.

Synthesis of impacts

Box 5.3. Subsidies, costs recovery and water management

Tariff increases for irrigation are expected and deemed both necessary and acceptable. However, given the expected need to support the agricultural sector, the systematic allocation of new revenue to other purposes is questionable.

More cost recovery of irrigation services opens up several policy choices. On the one hand, inefficient water use could continue to be subsidised. On the other, new resources could be redirected to support the uptake of water-efficient technologies (and, more generally, water-saving practices in the sector). A more financially autonomous irrigation network opens opportunities to redirect and target subsidies for a more comprehensive and effective water management policy.

Source: Authors' own work.

The social and environmental impacts of the proposed reform tend to be positive. However, there might be a small, but manageable negative economic impact, in the medium term. Affordability seems to be less of an issue, given the estimated willingness of farmers to pay for irrigation water.

In addition, however, reduced public subsidies by the state irrigation system may generate social and economic benefits. Specifically, this could free up significant public funds for both capital investment in rehabilitation and extension of water infrastructure, as well as the support system for specific groups (such as vulnerable households and farmers) and other socio-economic priorities. Other considerations are highlighted in Box 5.4. Furthermore, potential indirect effects, such as the marginal impacts of the proposed reform on food prices, need to be addressed. As water resource management improves, water supply for irrigation would become more reliable and resilience to the impacts of climate change and climate variability would increase.

Box 5.4. **Linking the fixed costs part of the proposed tariff to the current land tax system**

Under the current Tax Code, land tax is levied and collected by local authorities. Land-tax rates are already differentiated in KR (see next section), with higher tax rates for irrigated land than for non-irrigated land. As the proposed reform suggests adding the fixed costs part of the irrigation tariff to the land tax, it seems to propose double taxation.

In fact, irrigated land is not taxed twice, but only once through the land tax. This tax reflects the potential value of the land given its location and access to irrigation, but not its actual use. In turn, the fixed part of the irrigation tariff reflects the use of irrigation services through the user's commitment. The land tax instrument relates to the potential use of the land, and the irrigation tariff relates to the commitment to use irrigation services. Actual use of irrigation water would be paid through the variable part of the fee. Furthermore, land tax currently does not take into account the availability or absence of collector drainage system, although its availability increases the value of irrigated land.

Therefore, under the proposed reform, differentiated land-tax rates should take into account the aforementioned considerations.

Source: Based on authors' own work.

The expected impacts of the proposed scenarios are summarised in Table 5.4.

Table 5.4. **Reform of the level and structure of irrigation tariffs**

Synthesis of the expected impacts of the scenarios for reform

	Impact compared to current situation	Scenario 0	Scenario Ia	Scenario Ib	Scenario IIb	Scenario IIa
Economic and fiscal impacts	Businesses	0	0	0/-	0/-	0
	Innovation and research	0	0	+	+/0	+
	Consumers and households	0/-	0/-	0/-	0/-	0/-
	Public budget	+	+	+	++	++
	Water utilities and irrigation service providers	+	+	+	++	++
	Specific regions or sectors	0	-/0	-/0	-/0	-
	Overall impact	+	+/0	0/+	+/0	+

Table 5.4. **Reform of the level and structure of irrigation tariffs** *(continued)*

	Impact compared to current situation	Scenario 0	Scenario Ia	Scenario Ib	Scenario IIb	Scenario IIa
Social impacts	Vulnerable groups*	0	0	0/-	0/-	0/-
	Participation	0	0	+	+	+
	Public health and safety	0	0	0	0	0
	Overall impact	0	0	0/+	0/+	0
Environmental impacts	Climate	0	0	0	+	++
	Water quantity	0	0	0	0/+	0/+
	Water quality	0	0	0	0	0
	Water resources	0	0	0	0	0/+
	Overall impact	+/0	+/0	0/+	+	+

*Based on the assumption that eventual losses of vulnerable groups (households, small farmers) will be compensated from the strengthened social support system.

Source: Based on authors' own assessment.

Support and accompanying measures

A series of measures have been identified as prerequisites to provide the enabling environment for reform of irrigation tariffs and to enhance its acceptability in rural areas.

Medium term:

- Adopt regulation on introduction of the two-part irrigation tariff.
- Link introduction of irrigation tariff to broader agriculture improvement programmes focusing on more efficient practices (i.e. efficiency of energy, water use and inputs in general) to generated coherence and synergies between water management and key sector policies.
- Ensure co-ordination of irrigation tariff reforms with existing social support programmes targeted at vulnerable rural households.

Long term:

- Develop regulatory mechanisms that would ensure minimum environmental flows and orient any future water savings from agriculture to the aquifers or environmental needs in general.
- Continue to support uptake of water-efficient technologies in co-ordination with larger rural development programmes.

References

OECD (2013), *Improving the Use of Economic Instruments for Water Resource Management in Kyrgyzstan: the Case of Lake Issyk-Kul Basin*, EAP Task Force, OECD Publishing, Paris. www.oecd.org/environment/outreach/Kyrgyzstan_Eis%20for%20WRM_2nd%20edition_ENG%20web.pdf.

Chapter 6

Land taxes in the Lake Issyk-Kul area

Two scenarios for reform of land tax rate in the Lake Issyk-Kul area are assessed, and impacts of each scenario are synthesised in this chapter. Supporting and accompanying measures are proposed to facilitate implementation – these provide input to the draft Action Plan.

Context

Lake Issyk-Kul, the largest lake in Kyrgyzstan and in Central Asia, is also one of the largest mountain lakes in the world. It is located at an altitude of 1 606 m above sea level, with a surface area of 6 236 km^2; despite its high altitude, it never freezes, thanks to its salty water. Lake Issyk-Kul is between 668-702 m deep, and holds an estimated water volume of 1 738 km^3. It is 177 km long, with a maximum width of 60 km and a shore length of 597 km. Among all mountain lakes located over 1 200 m above sea level, Issyk-Kul is the largest in terms of water volume and depth; its water surface area is second in size only to Lake Titicaca in South America.

Lake Issyk-Kul's shoreline is endowed with an abundance of natural formations, which provide significant recreational and health benefits. The coastal area hosts around 20 types of natural landscapes with high recreational and aesthetic value.

The Issyk-Kul Oblast, given the status of Biosphere Reserve by the Law "On Biosphere Territories" (1999), is a protected area at the national level. There are two natural reserves on the territory of the oblast: the Issyk-Kul State Reserve and the Sarychat-Ertash Reserve with a total surface area of 149.1 ha, and the natural park Karakol (32 ha).

Data on land use in the Issyk-Kul Oblast are presented in Tables 6.1 and 6.2.

Table 6.1. **Land resources in the Issyk-Kul Oblast**

No.	Name of land categories	Total surface area (ha)	Including irrigated area (ha)
1	**Total land area (land for agricultural purposes)**	**731 069**	**138 328**
2	Total land use by settlements	33 209	13 149
3	Total land use for industry, transport, communication, defence, etc.	53 125	166
4	Total land area of special protected natural territories	43 795	171
5	Total land area of state forest resources	372 621	933
6	Total surface area of surface water bodies	630 258	-
7	Reserve lands	2 509 438	1 878
	Total land area in the oblast:	**4 373 515**	**154 625**
8	Land used outside of the oblast's administrative border	70 119	652
9	Lands used by land users from other oblasts	11 004	654
	Total land area within the oblast's jurisdiction	**4 314 400**	**154 627**

Source: State Statistics Committee of the Kyrgyz Republic.

Despite the large recreational and touristic potential, the main activity in the Issyk-Kul Oblast is agriculture, which primarily involves cattle breeding. However, the lack of availability of fresh water resources hinders the development of agriculture in the region.

The land-tax rate (per ha or per m^2) in Kyrgyzstan depends on the location and use of the land plot. The statutory land-tax rates set for agricultural land located in different regions (oblasts) of Kyrgyzstan are presented in Box 6.1; land tax for the use of garden plots next to houses, homestead plots and vegetable gardens plots appear in Box 6.2; and land-tax rates for the use of land in settlements and non-agricultural lands are outlined in Box 6.3.

Table 6.2. **Distribution of land resources of the Issyk-Kul Oblast, by type of use**

Land-use type	Total area, ha	Including irrigated area, ha
Arable land	190 613	133 766
Perennial plants	4 921	4 580
Grassland	14 246	1 840
Fallow land	1 683	-
Pastures	1 378 435	-
Total agricultural land area	**1 589 898**	**140 186**
Homestead lands (*land plots attached to private houses*)	22 697	12 146
Collective gardens	274	36
Collective vegetable gardens	768	631
Lands at the stage of reclamation construction	2 028	
Forest areas	117 766	722
Wood-and-shrubby plantations	48 978	906
Other lands	2 531 991	4 193
Total land area in use	**4 314 400**	**154 627**

Source: State Statistics Committee of the Kyrgyz Republic.

Box 6.1. **Basic land tax rates for the use of agricultural land**

1. Basic land-tax rates for the use of agricultural land are outlined in the table below.

	Land tax basic rates (KGS/hectare)				
Name of rayons (Issyk-Kul Oblast)	Arable land (irrigated)	Arable land (not irrigated)	Perennial vegetation	Grassland	Pasture
Ak-Suy Rayon	373	87.5	73	30.4	10.0
Djeti-Oguz Rayon	305	74.9	168	23.8	7.7
Issyk-Kul Rayon	280	68.6	155	23.8	7.7
Ton Rayon	236	39.2	119	20.4	7.1
Tyup Rayon	379	87.5	174	29.1	15.0

2. Basic land-tax rates for the use of agricultural land in cities and settlements are set at the rates specified by Part 1 of this Article, and shall be applied to the surrounding administrative rayon.
3. Basic land-tax rates for the use of water bodies are set at the rates specified by Part 1 of this Article, and shall be applied to irrigated land of the relevant rayon.
4. Basic land-tax rates for the use of lands irrigated by pumping stations are set at the rates specified in Part 1 of this Article, and shall be applied to dry arable land of the relevant rayon.
5. For agricultural land within settlements, classified by the Parliament of the Kyrgyz Republic as mountainous and remote areas, upon payment of the land tax for the use of agricultural land, benefits are set at the amount of 50% of the basic rate of the land tax for the given rayon.

Rayon councils have the right to increase the basic rate of land tax for the use of agricultural land, taking into account the fertility of the soil, as well as degradation of agricultural land. Except in cases of force majeure, this increase cannot be applied more than once per calendar year and more than three times.

Source: Tax Code of the Kyrgyz Republic (excerpts from Chapter 49. Land-tax rates. "Tax Code of the Kyrgyz Republic" as of 17 October,2008, No. 230. Article 337).

Formula for calculating land tax:

1. For agricultural land:

H = C x P x Ki, where:

H – amount of land tax, C – statutory rate of land tax, P – land area, in ha or m^2, Ki – inflation index.

2. For the land within settlements and non-agricultural land:

H = C x P x Ki x Kz x Kк, where:

H – amount of land tax, C – land tax rate, P – land area (m^2), Ki – inflation index, Kz and Kk – special coefficients set by the Law (Kz – zonal coefficient (*зональный коэффициент*) and Kk – the "coefficient of commercial use" – see the Tax Code of the Kyrgyz Republic for detail).

3. For garden plots next to houses, homestead and vegetable garden plots:

H = C x P x Kz, where:

H – amount of land tax, C – land tax rate, P – land area (m^2), Kz – zonal coefficient (*зональный коэффициент*). When the relevant coefficient has not been set, it is assumed to be equal to 1.0.

The Government of the Kyrgyz Republic approves the annual coefficient of inflation no later than 1 April of the current year, based on data from the previous year. If the coefficient of inflation is not set, it is assumed to be equal to the coefficient of the previous year.

In 2010, land tax revenue in the Issyk-Kul Oblast was as follows:[3]

1. For use of agricultural land: KGS 32 877 300
2. For use of garden plots next to houses, homestead and vegetable garden plots: KGS 16 389 900
3. For use of land in settlements and non-agricultural land: KGS 76 929 100.

Box 6.2. Land tax for garden plots next to houses, homestead plots and vegetable garden plots

1. Land-tax rates for the use of garden plots next to houses, homestead plots and vegetable garden plots, are set as follows:

Settlements	Land tax rate (KGS/m²)
1. Bishkek and Osh Cities	1.5
2. Towns of Tokmok, Kara-Balta, Djalal-Abad, Karakol, Talas, Cholpon-Ata	1.0
3. Towns not specified by Items 1 and 2 of the current table, and urban settlements, with the exception of rural settlements	0.5
4. Rural settlements	0.1

2. If the garden plots next to houses, homestead plot and/or vegetable garden plots or any part of them are used for business purposes, then the land tax for these lands is applied as a function of the coefficient of commercial use (Kk).

Source: Tax Code of the Kyrgyz Republic. Article 338.

Box 6.3. **Land-tax rates for use of land in settlements and non-agricultural lands**

1. Land-tax rates for use of land in settlements and non-agricultural lands are as follows:

	Land-tax rates in settlements with population, per '000 people (KGS/m²)							
Name of oblast	**Less than 5**	**From 5 to 10**	**From 10 to 20**	**From 20 to 50**	**From 50 to 100**	**From 100 to 200**	**From 200 to 500**	**500 and more**
Batken Oblast	0.9	1.4	1.5	1.7	1.7			
Djalal-Abad Oblast	1.2	1.6	1.8	2.0	2.1			
Issyk-Kul Oblast	**1.2**	**1.6**	**1.8**	**2.0**	**2.1**			
Naryn Oblast	1.0	1.4	1.6	1.7	1.8			
Osh Oblast	1.3	1.6	1.8	2.0	2.3	2.4	2.6	
Talas Oblast	1.1	1.5	1.7	1.9				
Chui Oblast and Bishkek City	1.2	1.6	1.8	2.0	2.3	2.4		2.9

2. For non-agricultural land outside the boundaries of settlements specified by Part 1 of this Article, the rates applied are those for settlements with a population between 5 100 to 10 000 people of the relevant rayon.
3. Land-tax rates are set by Part 1 of the given Article, and are differentiated by applying the zonal coefficient for economic-planning zones Kz and the coefficient of commercial use of land areas Kk.
4. The value of the zonal coefficient Kz is established by local councils, depending on special features of the economic-planning zones of settlements. It ranges between 0.3 to 1.2, can be set no more than once a year and no later than October 1st of the current year.

Source: Tax Code of the Kyrgyz Republic. Article 339.

Tax benefits

The following groups are exempt from land-tax payment for use of garden plots next to houses, homestead and vegetable garden plots:

1. Persons with disabilities and participants of the Second World War (Great Patriotic War); soldiers who participated under interstate agreements in the war in Afghanistan and in other countries; victims of the accident on the Chernobyl nuclear power plant; disabled individuals of groups I and II; and individuals disabled since childhood.
2. Members of the soldiers' family and of law enforcement officers, who were killed or missing during the performance of official duties, including minors.
3. Individuals who have reached retirement age.
4. Individuals who have four children or more.

Local councils have the right to grant full or partial exemption from land-tax payment for agricultural land for up to three years if the land user has suffered financial losses due to *force majeure*.

Rationale for reform

The presence of tourist activities in the protected area creates anthropogenic pressure and generates significant risks for water resources in the Lake Issyk-Kul area. These risks are due to inadequate infrastructure for the collection and disposal of solid waste, as well as lack of treatment and adequate discharge of wastewater from resorts and hotels.

The shore of Lake Issyk-Kul holds significant benefits for recreation and tourism, and the lake was awarded the status of protected natural area according to the Law "On Biosphere Reserve". These facts, however, were not taken into account in establishing land-tax rates. In other words, the existing land-tax system and cadastral prices (value) of property in the vicinity of Lake Issyk-Kul do not consider the **environmental and recreational value** of the Lake Issyk-Kul area. The main difficulty associated with revising the area's land-tax structure is the risk of creating an additional burden for affected taxpayers.

The summer tourist season lasts between three to four months. In 2012, it attracted about 1 156 000 tourists[2] (out of approximately 3 million registered for the country[3]), or about 4 times the size of the local population. Hence, Lake Issyk-Kul hosts an increasing number of **tourist facilities**. On the territory of Issyk-Kul Oblast, there are 370 facilities dedicated to tourism and recreation, and 26 resorts. Hotel services provided by the private sector are widely developed in the Issyk-Kul Oblast. The gross revenue of the recreation and tourism sector in the area amounts to KGS 298.4 million, which is 3.8 times more than in 2008 (KGS 78.4 million). Between 2008-12, the gross revenue of the hotel industry increased by 40% in nominal terms (from KGS 195.8 million to 276.7 million [NSC, 2013]). A recent survey of the Issyk-Kul region (SIAR, 2013) indicated that tourists spent around 20-26% of their overall budget on accommodation, which represented on average KGS 1 500 (tourists from the Russian Federation) or KGS 2 330 (tourists not from the Commonwealth of Independent States) – see Annex D, Tables D.12 and D.13 for details. This indicates the reported figures probably underestimate the revenue generated by the tourism sector in the area.

Tourism facilities are mostly owned and operated by private companies that are not necessarily based in the Lake Issyk-Kul area. Thus, local communities may only partially benefit from tourism, while the land-tax and land-lease systems are the main sources of income for local public administrations.

Objectives and principles of the proposed reform

The main objective of the reform is to **stimulate and promote better water management and the protection of aquatic ecosystems in the Lake Issyk-Kul area**, while creating additional financial resources for local communities, to be used for improved water management and ecosystem protection measures (such as proper municipal waste management).

The proposed reform aims to address the financial constraints experienced by local communities and local public budgets.

Since the Lake Issyk-Kul area's natural and recreational benefits are valuable to local land users (i.e. local communities and tourism operators), land users should contribute to water management and aquatic ecosystem protection in the area. With this in mind, the proposed scenarios below call for reform of the land and property tax. The basic principle of the scenarios is to link land use, water management and ecosystem protection in the Lake Issyk-Kul area.

Reform scenarios

- **Scenario I**: Targeted increase of contribution of hotel and recreational land users by 50% in the Lake Issyk-Kul area. This option targets the seasonal population of tourists, even if it relates to the former "hotel and resort tax", scrapped in the last reform of the Tax Code.
- **Scenario II**: Current land-tax rates are increased by 30%.

Table 6.3. **Land-tax reform: Proposed scenarios**

Timeline	Current situation	Short term: Scenario I Focused increase on tourism-related land uses by 50%	Medium term: Scenario II Increase of land-tax revenue by 30%
Description and objective	The current land-tax system differentiates between land uses and even between irrigated and rain-fed agriculture. Different coefficients in the formula of the land tax make this differentiation operational. However, the environmental and recreation value of the Lake Issyk-Kul area are not accounted for in the current system.	As the Lake Issyk-Kul area's natural and recreational benefits are valuable to local land users, tourism-related land users should contribute to water management and aquatic ecosystem protection measures in the area. This option targets tourism-related land owners.	As the Lake Issyk-Kul area's natural and recreational benefits are valuable to local land users (including local land and property owners, and tourism operators), all land users should contribute to water management and aquatic ecosystem protection measures in the area. This option targets all land owners.
Tax rate	Detailed coefficients for agricultural land (irrigated and rain-fed), as well as settlements and gardens.	Tax rates would be increased for each land plot based on the oblast's cadaster to account for the high value of land in the Lake Issyk-Kul area. The increase in land plot prices is calculated through a specific formula: a +50% increase is applied to land-tax rates for tourism operators.	Tax rates would be increased for each land plot based on the oblast's cadaster to account for the high value of land in the Lake Issyk-Kul area. The increase in land plot prices is calculated through a specific formula: a +30% increase is applied to current land-tax rates.
Tax base	As above	Updated land plot prices, obtained by increasing the zoning coefficients associated to each target group in the Lake Issyk-Kul area.	
Revenue allocation	Revenue will continue to be allocated to local communities, but will be differentiated: the oblast's general budget will continue to receive the same revenue as under current land-tax rates. Additional revenue generated by the reform will be earmarked and used by local communities for water management and for the protection of aquatic ecosystems.		
Coherence with existing legislation	In coherence with the current tax law.	Modification to the Tax Code and sub-laws governing land tax will be necessary.	

Source: Based on authors' own findings.

Additional revenue obtained through the reform will be reinvested in water management and protection of aquatic ecosystem in the Lake Issyk-Kul area, as outlined in Table 6.4.

Table 6.4. **Revenue implications of the proposed scenarios for Issyk-Kul Oblast**

Revenue (mln KGS)	Agricultural land	Gardens	Settlements	Total
Collected in 2010	32.9	16.4	76.9	126.2
Potential revenue after land-tax rate increase of 50% for tourism-related land use*	32.9	16.4	78.7	128.0
Potential Increase of land-tax rate by 30%	42.8	21.3	100	164.1

* Assuming 139 hotels and 370 enterprises of tourism and recreation, with a conservative estimate of 1 ha of taxed surface.

Source: Adapted form authors' own findings.

Expected impacts

In terms of impacts, each scenario brings similar, although gradually evolving results.

Scenario I

Most of the 139 hotels and 370 tourism-related companies registered in the Issyk-Kul area will have to contribute to the proposed increased land-tax rates. This cost, however, can be passed onto tourists so they can also actively contribute to improved water management.

Additional revenue generated by the instrument can be earmarked for innovative projects that improve water management. The instrument will not promote greater productivity or water resources efficiency, although some pilot projects might be launched that could result in less water pollution.

Land-tax breaks could provide incentives for facilities that demonstrate best practice in handling wastewater; they could be exempted from the proposed tax rate increase, which would contribute to reducing pollution discharges.

Scenario II

Additional revenue generated (30%) would be earmarked and used by the oblast and local public authorities to improve water management and protect aquatic ecosystems. Some minor administrative costs would be linked to earmarking these funds; however, they will likely be less than the proceeds of the increased land tax.

Since the instrument will generate additional revenue, the additional funds can be used to finance innovative projects. The instrument itself does not directly promote greater productivity or resource efficiency. However, some relevant pilot projects might be supported in the territories where scarcity of water resources is an issue.

In 2012, according to the NSC (2013), all taxes and fees levied represented 6% of the average income per capita for the Issyk-Kul Oblast (the average was 7.8% and 5.4% in urban and rural areas respectively). A 30% increase of land tax would therefore remain affordable for the average household.

Although there are no specific data to prove it, the proposed 30% increase could create affordability issues for social groups with the lowest income. The land tax is expected to have a larger impact on the poor as they depend heavily on subsistence farming rather than on regular incomes, and only have land as a safety net.

However, the extremely poor may be proportionally less affected than the poor as they only have very limited access to land.[4] Moreover, the percentage of tax-related expenditure is lower in rural than in urban areas, as outlined above.

Local governments would use the extra revenue generated by the reform for water management and protection of aquatic ecosystems. This would improve public awareness of sustainable water use and ecosystem protection.

Thanks to pilot environmental projects to improve water quality and overall environmental quality, the proposed instrument will decrease the likelihood of health risks in the Issyk-Kul area. It is unlikely that small-scale pilot projects would significantly contribute to climate change adaptation. Financing improved water management practices, including respecting the regime of sanitary protection zones for drinking water sources, will contribute to the protection of drinking water quality.

Synthesis of impacts

This synthesis highlights that both scenarios are expected to deliver positive social and environmental impacts. Thus implementation of both scenarios would likely have a positive impact.

However, Scenario I is more comprehensive and accounts for two important factors:

- All users are generating pressure on the lake, not just seasonal tourists.
- Formal hotels and tourism enterprises only host a share of tourists. Many local residents open their homes as guest houses and therefore share the burden of responsibility with respect to water quality of the lake.

That said, Scenario II is less likely to raise specific affordability concerns; additional costs are expected to be passed onto tourists, who by definition have a proven willingness to pay for accommodation in the area.

The expected impacts of the proposed scenarios are summarised in Table 6.5.

Table 6.5. **Synthesis of the expected impacts of the scenarios for land-tax reform**

	Impact compared to current situation	Scenario I	Scenario II
Economic and fiscal impacts	Businesses	0/-	0/-
	Innovation and research	0/+	0/+
	Consumers and households	0/-	-
	Public budget	+/0	+
	Water utilities and irrigation service providers	+/0	+/0
	Specific regions or sectors	-/0	-
	Overall impact	0/-	0/-
Social impacts	Vulnerable groups	0	-
	Participation	+/0	+
	Public health and safety	0/+	0/+
	Overall impact	0/+	0/-

Table 6.5. **Synthesis of the expected impacts of the scenarios for land-tax reform** *(continued)*

	Impact compared to current situation	Scenario I	Scenario II
Environmental impacts	Climate	0	0/+
	Water quantity	0/+	0/+
	Water quality	0/+	+
	Water resources	+	+
	Overall impact	0/+	+

Source: Based on authors' own assessments.

Support and accompanying measures

A series of measures have been identified as prerequisites to provide the enabling environment for a reform of land-tax rates in Lake Issyk-Kul area and enhance its political acceptability in the region.

Short-term measures *(for Scenario II):*

- Amendments to the legislation to revise basic tax rates for land use in settlements, with a specific rate for land use by tourism and recreational infrastructure; and differentiating tax rates depending on availability of water infrastructure (WSS; storm water collection; protection from floods, mud flows and groundwater flooding) on the territory of the Issyk-Kul Biosphere reserve area.

Medium-term measures *(for Scenario I):*

- Amendments to the legislation to revise basic tax rates for land use for agriculture, gardens and settlements; and differentiating tax rates depending on the availability of water infrastructure (WSS; storm water collection; protection from flood, mud flow and groundwater flooding) in Kyrgyzstan.

Notes

1. Data of the Ministry of Finance of the Kyrgyz Republic.
2. According to the Issyk-Kul Oblast State Administration.
3. NSC, 2011 in SIAR, 2013. According to SIAR (2013), official sources do not reflect the actual situation in the sector. There is a problem with definition of the notion of "a tourist", which (currently) does not distinguish between real tourists and the Kyrgyz labour migrants who changed their citizenship and visit the country for private purposes.
4. This hypothesis was inspired by Nippon Koei (2009a and 2009b).

References

National Statistical Committee of the Kyrgyz Republic (2013), *Statistical Yearbook,* NCS, Bishkek.

National Statistical Committee of the Kyrgyz Republic (2013), *Tourism in Kyrgyzstan 2008-12,* NSC, Bishkek.

National Statistical Committee of the Kyrgyz Republic (2011), *Statistical Yearbook,* NCS, Bishkek.

Nippon Koei Co. Ltd, and RAM Engineering Associates (2009a), "City level infrastructure plan (CLIP), Cholpon Ata, Issyk-Kul sustainable development project", Kyrgyz Republic, *Report ADB TA NO. 7228 KGZ*, Volume 1, Bishkek.

Nippon Koei Co. Ltd, and RAM Engineering Associates (2009b), "Social assessment, Cholpon Ata, Issyk-Kul sustainable development project", Kyrgyz Republic, *Report ADB TA NO. 7228 KGZ,* Volume 8, Bishkek.

SIAR (2013), "Survey of tourism market in Kyrgyzstan. Report to the USAID Local Development Program", Social and Marketing Research Centre, Baku City.

Chapter 7

Cholpon-Ata city case study on water supply and sanitation tariffs

Preferred scenarios for reform of water supply and sanitation tariffs are often site-specific. For Cholpon-Ata city, two scenarios for reform of water supply and sanitation tariffs are assessed, and impacts of each scenario are synthesised in this chapter. Supporting and accompanying measures are proposed to facilitate implementation – these provide input to the draft Action Plan. Some of the measures are quite universal and could be applied also in other settlements.

Rationale for reform

The water utility of the town of Cholpon Ata is an interesting case because of its location on the shoreline of Lake Issyk-Kul,[1] and the current structure of tariff for water supply and sanitation, which leaves much room for improvement. The town, located in the Issyk Kul Oblast, is the capital of the eponymous rayon. It is relatively small with a permanent population of 12 000-16 000 people. However, this population almost doubles during the summer tourist season. The town is an attractive area with numerous publicly-owned and privately-operated resorts on Lake Issyk-Kul.

Part of the town relies on groundwater from 15 boreholes for water supply; the remaining part is supplied by surface water from the River Aral, therefore complicating logistics.

In 2009, only 39% of surveyed households in the town received sufficient water for their domestic needs (Nippon Koei, 2009b).

Another important aspect of WSS in the town and surrounding areas is the prevalence of water-borne infections (WBI), which constitute a burden for poor households, and lead to:

- high treatment costs (KGS 1 450 per household per annum, on average, for all households)
- lost school days (10 days per annum lost by each children from poor households)
- loss of labour productivity.

The water supply tariff structure is volumetric, with two distinct levels according to the source of the water supplied. The tariff is lower for surface water than for groundwater sources (due to pumping costs). In turn, wastewater treatment is also subject to a tariff to cover treatments costs. The structure of tariffs also distinguishes domestic and industrial uses (see Table 7.1).

After years of substantial tariff increases, and following political instability in 2010, tariffs for water supply and sanitation were lowered to 2007 levels. Based on the tariffs

Table 7.1. **Tariffs for WSS services charged by the Cholpon-Ata Water Utility (effective since 2010)**

Categories	Unit	Tariff
Water supply service		
Residential users		
a. Customers connected to gravity-fed WS system from surface water source	KGS/m³	*3.5*
b. Customers connected to WS system fed from groundwater source	KGS/m³	*6.5*
Industrial users		
a. Customers connected to gravity-fed WS system from surface water source	KGS/m³	*10*
b. Customers connected to WS system fed from groundwater source	KGS/m³	*19*
Sanitation (sewerage) service		
Residential users	*KGS/m³*	*8.5*
Industrial users	*KGS/m³*	*23*

Source: Cholpon Ata Vodokanal.

detailed in Table 7.1, water supply tariffs paid by water users fall short of covering O&M costs; the municipality effectively subsidises over 30% of water supply costs. Overall, the utility runs a deficit of 15%, when taking into account the sewage treatment costs coverage (Cholpon Ata Vodokanal). Cholpon Ata's sewerage network is limited and the current level of sanitation and wastewater treatment is quite low (i.e. only 35% of houses connected to water supply are also connected to the collective (centralised) sewerage system; present sanitation tariffs cover O&M costs and even generate some surplus. Due to low sanitation coverage, most resorts and hotels have installed their own local wastewater treatment plants (LWWTPs), but such installations are not reported to be functioning well, if at all. Moreover, the utility does not have access to the resorts to monitor and inspect LWWTPs (Nippon Koei et al., 2009a).

Box 7.1. **Affordability of water tariffs**

Affordability is usually measured by the affordability index, which compares the average household's bill for water supply and sanitation services to its disposable income. Households are generally considered to be in "water poverty" when the affordability index is higher than 3%; however, this upper threshold can be set between 1-3% depending on policy choices (Smets, 2008). The affordability index must be calculated with respect to the average household's disposable income, but also with respect to the disposable income of low-income households (e.g. lowest income quintile). In transition countries, the average affordability index of low-income groups is generally estimated to be between 3-7%. An affordability index of 6% is normally considered the upper affordability threshold for low-income groups: beyond this upper limit, measures are required to make access to water and sanitation services affordable (Smets, 2008).

Source: Adapted from Smets (2008).

Moreover, it has been reported that tourists are not only hosted in formal establishments, but also in informal guesthouses run by the local population. Half of households are estimated to host tourists during summer, generating additional pressure on the centralised sewerage network, although most of the formal tourism establishments are not connected.

The proportion of household income spent on WSS services varies between urban and rural households and depends on the household's income. In this case, *(i)* household incomes tend to be somewhat under-reported, particularly in rural areas; and *(ii)* the billed services tend to over-report actual payments, due to low collection rates (OECD, 2011a). The OECD estimated that prior to the 2008 economic crisis, the share of household income spent on water services in Kyrgyzstan was around 0.9% (OECD, 2011b). As indicated earlier, water bills are the lowest from all utility services, representing on average about 1.2% of disposable income in 2009 (CIS Statistics Committee, 2011). More recent samples (for 2011 and 2012) indicate that water bills represent between 1.2-6% of the disposable income of the lowest quintile of households in several provincial towns. Therefore, doubling or tripling current tariffs in real terms (accounting for inflation) are expected to have a significant impact for a fraction of the poorest households. Water and sanitation services only represent about 0.2% to 0.7% of the disposable income of the wealthier households (see Annex D, pages 120 to 123: Recent sample of the water bill expenditure to income ratio in regional cities across Kyrgyzstan [in 2011 and 2012]).

These tariffs are low by regional and international standards; there may be scope for increases without making the service unaffordable to most users. If the 2008 crisis had not eroded the willingness to pay in Kyrgyzstan, the affordability threshold set at 2.5% by the NPD on WSS in Kyrgyzstan (OECD, 2011b) might still be valid. Box 7.1 above provides further explanation on affordability for water and sanitation services.

A 2008 household survey in the Issyk-Kul Oblast indicated a marked interest of the population to be provided with, and to pay for, improved water supply and sanitation (see Table 7.2).

Table 7.2. **Willingness to pay (WTP) data for improved water supply and sanitation**

Oblast	WTP for improved water supply			WTP for improved sanitation			
	WTP for reliable tap water supply KGS/person/month	**WTP more for water supply to home**		Percentage of households willing to pay for a hygienic toilet	Average lump sum households are willing to pay for quality toilet, KGS	Highest reported WTP for toilet (lump sum), KGS	Percentage of households willing to pay KGS 8 000 for a hygienic toilet
		Percentage of households	KGS/person/ month				
Issyk Kul	15.8	100	26.8	95	2 479	10 000	78

Source: (OECD, 2011a).

In turn, a 2009 survey (Nippon Koei et al., 2009b) showed that a little less than half of the households surveyed (43.6%) paid for water supply services in Cholpon Ata. Although 58% of households said they would be willing to pay for improved water supply infrastructure and 49% for sanitation, 73% stated they were not prepared to pay more than they currently did. A quarter of households surveyed were prepared to pay up to 25% more than current contributions, and only 1% were willing to pay up to 50% more. The poorest households were willing to connect to the sewerage network, but 44% of them were not willing to pay for the connection.

The proposed reform in a nutshell

The proposed reform of this instrument would pursue the following objectives:

Short term: Increase financial revenue earmarked to strengthen the administrative capacity of Vodokanals required for sustainable water management, recovery of O&M costs, adequate monitoring and control, reporting, and research and development.

Medium- to long-term: Significantly contribute to the **full recovery of the costs** of WSS services (including O&M costs; partial and total capital costs, including the rehabilitation costs of existing infrastructure). Environmental costs are not yet estimated. To reach this objective, several reform scenarios were considered. In addition to gradual increases of the tariff, a shift to a two-part tariff system (see Box 7.2) was also explored.

Based on these considerations, the following reform scenarios were developed:

- **Scenario I**: A gradual increase in tariff rates, keeping current tariff structure and service levels.
- **Scenario II**: Introduction of a two-part tariff to ensure sustainable financing of WSS services and to mobilise more financial resources to substantially improve service levels by 2025.

Box 7.2. **Introducing a two-part water supply and sanitation tariff**

Under the proposed reform, the first part of the water tariff would be set to contribute to the fixed costs. This part is to be collected on the basis of a network connection and independently of water-use levels.

The second part of the tariff would cover the variable cost of providing water supply services. This would cover energy costs, such as electricity bills for pumping water, which represent one of the largest expenditure items for the *Vodokanal* of Cholpon Ata. These costs vary according to the volume of water supplied to users; therefore, it is appropriate that a volumetric charge is applied (per m^3 of water). The volumetric charge could also include an additional fee to account for the use of water as a natural resource (see above section on surface water-use charges), as a means of providing an incentive for water-use efficiency.

Source: Based on authors' own findings.

Table 7.3. **Proposed scenarios for the reform of water supply and sanitation tariffs**

Timeline	Current situation	Medium term: Scenario I A gradual increase in tariff rates, keeping current tariff structure	Medium- to long-term: Scenario II A structural change of the tariff system to substantially improve service levels by 2025
Description and objective	The municipal budget effectively subsidises more than 30% of the costs of supplying water. The utility runs a financial deficit of 15%, when the costs of providing sanitation services are included.	Vodokanals no longer depend on subsidies. Under the proposed scheme, around 5% of the city budget is freed up for other purposes. Present tariffs cover current O&M costs, but not the costs of rehabilitating expanded services.	This scenario assumes that *(i)* up to 90% of the population is connected to water supply (from the current 83%) and to the sewerage network (from the current 35%), *(ii)* non-revenue water is reduced to 20% (from the current 82.9%), corresponding to the good practices in some cities in EECCA; and *(iii)* meters are systematically installed. Investments for these changes would need support from the state or donor agencies in the form of a viability gap fund (VGF). But the proposed tariffs would cover the costs of full O&M, debt servicing and interests.
Tariff rates	As indicated in Table 7.1 above.	An increase of 32.6% of the differentiated tariffs over five years (i.e. 4-5% per year). This is line with the timeframe of the National Sustainable Development Strategy for 2013-17 for the Kyrgyz Republic.	Introduction of a two-part tariff and an increase of differentiated tariffs, once the first investments are implemented: the tariff would include: *(i)* a fixed cost component, covering fixed costs of WSS services + water management costs; and *(ii)* rate per m^3. The variable part of the tariff is increased by 4-5% every year to fully cover the costs of O&M by 2025.
Tariff base	In principle, tariffs are based on volumetric water use. In practice, low metering means that water bills are calculated by multiplying the number of individuals in a connected by a "consumption norm". The size of households tends to be under-reported by residential customers.		Volumetric water use (variable component) and a fixed component, linked to the connection to water and sewerage networks.
Revenue allocation	As is currently the norm, revenue would be collected by the Vodokanal, and used according to its cost recovery strategy.		
Coherence with existing legislation	As pricing policy of water supply and sanitation services is guided by the state, tariffs are subject to approval by the town's municipal council or *Kenesh*, and concurred with the town's anti-monopoly committee (state representative for the regulation of pricing and tariffs).		

Source: Based on authors' own findings.

Table 7.4. **Full WSS management budget (in mln. KGS)**

	CURRENT Budget in 2010	**SCENARIO I (covers O&M)**	**SCENARIO II 2025 budget (covers O&M, debt servicing and interest rates) (in nominal prices)***		
Expected additional revenue (in mln. KGS)					
Source	Revenue in 2010	Expected revenue in five years	Fixed part (connection fee)	Variable part of tariff	Expected revenue in 2025 (nominal) (excluding VGF**)
Revised tariff structure, with tariffs rates increased by 4-5% per year (for water supply from groundwater)	4.522	5.996	*2.34*	*7.61*	9.948
Revised tariff structure, with tariffs rates increased by 4-5% per year (for water supply from surface water)	1.339	1.775	*0.73*	*2.21*	2.946
Current tariff structure, increased tariffs (for sanitation services)	4.634	4.634	*0.28*	*19.01*	19.296
Total	**10.495**	**12.406**			**32.189**

* This improved budget is based on the assumption that 10% more water supply connections will join the network and up to 90% of the population will be connected to the sewage network during 2014-25. This budget does not account for capital costs, only running costs. The higher revenue than O&M expenditure hints at the possibility of contributing to capital costs (i.e. debt servicing).

** **Viability Gap Funding (VGF)**: One-time or deferred grant to support infrastructure projects that are economically justified, but have short-term viability limitations.

Source: Based on authors' own assessment.

Expected impacts

In terms of impacts, the scenarios generate gradually increasing results, although there is a structural shift in the options with the introduction of the two-part tariff.

Scenario I

The most important impact of the proposed reform is the generation of additional revenue for the utility, which **in the long run**, is expected to fully cover O&M costs.

Thanks to the utility's reduced dependence on operational subsidies, the proportion of the municipal budget (around 5%) previously spent on water services can now be redirected to strengthen targeted social programmes.

Given *(i)* the currently low proportion of household disposable income spent on water services and *(ii)* the known willingness to pay for improved water supply, only marginal effects are expected in terms of affordability. The proposed tariff change could become a financial burden for the poorest households if the proportion of income spent on water services reaches 2.5%; however, it is unlikely at this level of tariff rates. By the same token, no significant changes in water usage are expected.

However, tariff changes require the approval of the municipal council (*Kenesh*) and this process may entail some transaction costs.

Scenario II

Affordability levels of water supply services are expected to change significantly, at least in nominal terms. Two aspects need to be highlighted: the increase in the water supply tariff and the expansion of sewerage services, meaning that an increased share of the population will be paying for a new service.

The costs of extended sanitation services are expected to have a negative impact on the poorest households. However, this would be compensated by a health benefit: in the short to medium term, as the incidence of water-borne infections decreases, households would enjoy lower medical bills (**immediate financial benefits**). In the longer term, larger **economic benefits** are associated with a healthier population and increased labour productivity (but assessing these long-term benefits is beyond the scope of this report).

As in Scenario I, the utility's reduced dependence on operational subsidies would allow the proportion of the municipal budget (around 5%) previously spent on water services to be redirected to strengthen targeted social programmes.

Water would be continuously available across the system, and higher tariffs are expected to provide incentives for more efficient use. This, in turn, would lead to lower energy use and reduce the expenditure associated with pumping costs.

The proposed tariff changes would require a local debate and approval by the municipal council (Kenesh), which is expected to be more intense than under Scenario I, and may entail higher transaction costs.

Synthesis of impacts

Under Scenario I, 5% of the municipal budget could be reallocated to other socio-economic priorities, as additional revenue would cover the current financial gap in the Vodolkanal's operations, while retaining current levels of services. As such, it is not very ambitious.

Scenario II is more ambitious as it includes the introduction of a two-part tariff and the enlargement of the number of households connecting to the sewerage network. The proposal has two implications that need to be highlighted: an increase in the tariff for water supply; and the expansion of sewerage services, meaning that a larger share of the population would be paying for a new service.

In terms of affordability, the tariff increase is significant in nominal terms over the period reviewed. The adoption of the new sanitation service would have to be closely monitored for the poorest segment of the population; it could have an effect in real terms on poor households' budgets that may require special support measures.

The expected impacts of the proposed scenarios are summarised in Table 7.5.

Table 7.5. **Reform of the level and structure of tariffs: Synthesis of expected impacts of the scenarios for reform**

	Impact compared to current situation	Scenario I	Scenario II
Economic and fiscal impacts	Businesses	0/-	0/-
	Innovation and research	0	+
	Consumers and households	0/-	-
	Public budget	+/0	++
	Water utilities and irrigation service providers	+/0	++
	Specific regions or sectors	+	0
	Overall impact	**0/+**	**+**
Social impacts	Vulnerable groups*	0/-	-
	Participation	0	+
	Public health and safety	+/0	+
	Overall impact	**0/-**	**0/+**
Environmental impacts	Climate	0	+
	Water quantity	+/0	+
	Water quality	0	+
	Water resources	0	+
	Overall impact	**+/0**	**+**

*Based on the assumption that eventual losses of vulnerable groups will be compensated from the strengthened social support system.

Source: Authors' own assessment.

Support and accompanying measures

A series of measures have been identified as prerequisites for the enabling environment needed to reform the WSS tariff rates and structure.

- Develop and implement a metering strategy, prioritising the installation of water meters and lowering levels of non-revenue water (i.e. water leakage control and collection rate improvement).
- Draft a proposal for Vodokanals' tariff changes for the 2025 horizon.
- Strengthen and build financial management capacity in Vodokanals, including that of financial officers and accountants.
- If the most vulnerable groups still cannot afford water supply services, provide additional support by limiting the tariff for both water supply and sanitation services to the fixed costs component under the given threshold, adequately monitored through metering. This measure requires the installation of individual meters.
- Subsidise network connections for all households. Related costs can then be gradually transferred to households, at least partially, given the willingness to pay for reliable piped water supply.

Note

1. This also contributes to the wider water-related economic instruments for WRM suggested for the Lake Issyk-Kul area.

References

Nippon Koei Co. Ltd, and RAM Engineering Associates (2009b), "Social assessment, Cholpon Ata, Issyk-Kul sustainable development project", Kyrgyz Republic, *Report ADB TA NO. 7228 KGZ,* Volume 8, Bishkek.

OECD (2011a), "Strengthening financial planning and management for WSS in central government, municipalities and utilities of EECCA countries", presentation on the national policy dialogue on financing strategy for urban and rural water supply and sanitation in the Kyrgyz Republic, Kiev, 24 April 2009, www.oecd.org/environment/outreach/42756430.pdf.

OECD (2011b), *Ten Years of Water Sector Reform in Eastern Europe, Caucasus and Central Asia*, OECD Publishing, Paris, http://dx.doi.org/10.1787/9789264118430-en.

Smets, H. (2008), *De l'eau potable à un prix abordable: La pratique des États,* Académie de l'eau, Nanterre.

Chapter 8

Introducing product taxes (including import duty) on selected products polluting water in Kyrgyzstan

Most point-source water pollutants are currently tackled by a range of pollution fees. However, this instrument is not effective for managing ***diffuse pollution****, when individual polluters cannot be identified or monitored. Examples of pollutants that most contribute to diffuse pollution of water resources in Kyrgyzstan include pesticides, mineral fertilisers and machinery lubricants with mineral oil. These are all prone to leaching and have contaminated both surface and groundwater without much control to date.*

Several scenarios for introducing product taxes and respective import duty on (a) *pesticide and other agricultural chemicals; and* (b) *on motor oil and other machinery lubricants are assessed, and impacts of each scenario are synthesised in this chapter. Supporting and accompanying measures are proposed to facilitate implementation – these provide input to the draft Action Plan.*

Pesticides

Agricultural chemicals, such as mineral fertilisers and pesticides, have various direct and indirect effects on both human and ecosystem health (Tauw, 2009). Among other impacts, they contribute to contamination of surface and ground water resources with phosphorus and nitrates; nitrates are subject to concentration control for drinking water sources, and if in high concentration (>45.0 mg/L[1]) raw water may require costly treatment or the use of alternative sources.

Prior to independence, Kyrgyzstan used about 5 000 tonnes of pesticides annually (around 30% of which were POPs pesticides), with an application rate up to 10 kg/ha. Peak use of POPs pesticides occurred in the 1970s and 1980s. In the late 1980s, chemical agents were used on around 1 million ha to grow cotton, sugar beets, vegetables, tobacco, grain crops, gardens, vineyards and pasture land.

Estimates of pesticide use in Kyrgyzstan are presented in Table 8.1, while Tables 8.2 and 8.3 present data on their total annual values and average prices, respectively.

Currently, pesticides used in Kyrgyzstan are entirely imported, and this product is exempt from VAT (article 255-256 of the Tax Code). This aims to help farmers access this agricultural input, but its usage remains an environmental challenge.

Following the independence of Kyrgyzstan and throughout the 1990s, the use of chemical inputs decreased dramatically (UNECE, 2009, 2000). Pesticide use is now less than 10% of what it was 25 years ago. It fell significantly on the onset of the 2008 crisis, with rates of application between 0.01 kg and 1 kg/ha.[2] The average pesticide load is currently estimated at 5 kg/ha of arable land (Kyrgyz Republic, 2007).

Table 8.1. **Estimated volume of used and discarted lubricants in Kyrgyzstan, tonnes per year**

Item/Year	2007	2008	2009	2010	2011
Insecticides	83.4	113.7	82.1	109.4	94.8
Herbicides	125.3	140.8	163.1	169.0	160.0
Fungicides and bactericides	817.5	408.3	21.6	71.7	58.1

Note: Based on population and estimated number of vehicles in 2010.

Source: Calculation by authors based on data from BIOS (2010) and NSC (2011).

Table 8.2. **Annual value of pesticides for agriculture imported in Kyrgyzstan, in USD thousands**

Item/Year	2008	2009	2010	2011	2012
Total value of imported pesticides	**4 674**	**5 522**	**6 885.75**	**8 983.23**	**10 654.84**
Hazardous pesticides	289		1.46	34.28	
Insecticides*	1 396	1 756	1 786.66	3 075.47	4 327.18
Fungicides*	439	572	869.9	990.77	804.03
Herbicides*	2 180	2 694	3 078.05	4 322.81	4 768.88
Disinfectants*	370	501	1 149.68	559.9	754.75

*Excluding hazardous pesticides.

Source: National Statistics Committee, adopted from FAO (2014).

Table 8.3. **Estimated nominal value of 1 kg of pesticide imported in Kyrgyzstan, in USD**

	2008	2009	2010	2011
Insecticides	14.82	21.39	16.35	32.80
Herbicides	15.48	16.52	18.21	27.02
Fungicides and bactericides	1.98	49.68	28.17	26.69

Note: Important variations can be seen between the early years and more recent data, probably due to accuracy of records. However, it is an indicator of the basic value of the products as tax base.

Source: Elaborated by authors based on data from Tables 8.1 and 8.2.

Lubricants

When disposed of after use, lubricants hold more polluting substances as they have accumulated a number of pollutants – from unused fuel to heavy metals from engines (Denton, 2007) – in addition to their suspected carcinogenic chemical compounds (i.e. polycyclic aromatic hydrocarbons [PAHs]).

Similarly to pesticides, all lubricants in KR are imported. It was not possible to identify the quantities of lubricants used every year in the country from available statistics and custom records. However, quantities that could be disposed of into the environment were estimated based on population and number of vehicles.

The analysis of a sample of 13 upper middle- to high-income countries in Europe (BIOIS, 2010), reveals that around 5 kg/capita of used oil are produced on average per year. When looking at the number of vehicles in the same sample, this weighted average is 8.8 kg/road motor vehicle.[3]

As these countries are wealthier, the total consumption of lubricants is expected to be higher than in Kyrgyzstan so the above weighted averages should be seen as a maximum. However, the age of vehicles in Kyrgyzstan is also higher, pointing at a potentially higher consumption per vehicle.

Assuming a population in Kyrgyzstan of about 5 607 000 inhabitants, the above ratio would indicate that a maximum of 28 554t of used oil are used and disposed of in the country every year. Using the ratio related to the number of motor vehicles, this estimate reaches a high of 7 984t (given the more than 900 000 vehicles registered in 2014[4]), and a low of 3 784t based on 419 000 vehicles officially registered in 2010, excluding motorbikes (2011 data from the National Statistical committee. For details, see Annex D.

Table 8.4. **Estimated volume of used and discarted lubricants in Kyrgyzstan, tonnes per year**

Estimates	Consumed lubricants and oils	Waste oils
Low estimates (based on registered vehicles in 2010)	7 737.2	3 784.6
High estimates (based on current number of vehicles registered)	16 323.2	7 984.4
Maximum estimate (based on population)	58 376.5	28 554.7

Note: Based on population and estimated number of vehicles in 2010.

Source: Calculation by authors based on data from BIOS (2010) and NSC (2011).

Rationale for reform

Pesticides

Although legislation lists authorised products, and measures for handling and storing chemicals (see Box 8.1), there are neither regulatory nor economic instruments to tackle diffuse pollution. This increases the environmental and health risks associated with such chemicals.

Box 8.1. **Current legislation on pesticides**

The following laws of the Kyrgyz Republic address the regulation of pesticides:

- On Sanitary and Epidemiological Welfare of Population
- On Chemicalisation and Protection of Plants
- On Environmental Protection
- On Atmospheric Air Protection.

The following decrees and acts of the Kyrgyz Republic address the regulation of pesticides:

- Resolution of the Government of the Kyrgyz Republic as of 27 July 2001 № 376 "On measures to protect the environment and population health from the adverse impacts of certain hazardous chemical substances and pesticides"
- List of pesticides and agricultural chemicals approved for use in the Kyrgyz Republic for 2000-04, published for five years by the State Department of Chemicalisation and Protection of Plants of the Ministry of Agriculture, Water Resources and Processing Industry of the Kyrgyz Republic
- Instructions for safe handling and storage of pesticides in agricultural production (approved by Order of Minister of Agriculture, Water Resources and Processing Industry of the Kyrgyz Republic as of 20 November 2001 № 309, registered in the Ministry of Justice of the Kyrgyz Republic, registration No. 206-01 as of 12 December 2001)
- SanPiN 1.2.1077-01 "Hygienic requirements for storage, application and transportation of pesticides and agrochemicals" (approved by the Resolution of the Chief State Sanitary Doctor of the Kyrgyz Republic as of 2 May 2003 № 31)
- SanPiN 1.1.002-03 "Hygienic requirements for the production of pesticides and agrochemicals" (approved by Resolution of the Chief State Sanitary Doctor of the Kyrgyz Republic as of 20 February 2004 No. 10, registered at the Ministry of Justice of the Kyrgyz Republic, registration No. 37-04 as of 19 March 2004)
- Hygienic standards for content of pesticides in environmental objects (list) (approved by Resolution of the Chief State Sanitary Doctor of the Kyrgyz Republic as of 28 May 2004 № 20, registered in the Ministry of Justice of the Kyrgyz Republic, registration No. 64-04 as of 10 June 2004)
- SanPiN 2.1.7.005-03 "Sanitary requirements for the quality of the soil" (approved by the Resolution of the Chief State Sanitary Doctor of the Kyrgyz Republic on 20 February 2004 number 9) and others.

Source: Kyrgyz Republic (2007), The National Plan for the implementation of the Stockholm Convention on persistent organic pollutants.

Lubricants

Re-use or recycling are effective ways to reduce the diffuse pollution from used lubricants (see Box 8.2).

Nevertheless, both options require existence of a cost-effective method for collection and recycling, or a re-use system supported by strong economic incentives for good performance.

Box 8.2. **Lubricants: Recycle or re-use?**

In general, to gain maximum energy conservation and environmental benefits, it is better to re-refine used oils into regenerated base oils that can then be blended into finished lube oil products; this is preferable to combustion of used oils for heating value recovery. A recent study found that re-refining used oils saves about 8% of the energy content of the used oil, compared to combusting the oil for heating purposes (DOE, 2006).

Re-refining oils can lead to additional environmental benefits because toxic heavy metals (e.g. zinc, lead, cadmium and chromium) are extracted from the used oils. These metal compounds are solidified and stabilised into asphalt flux, thereby posing minimal environmental risk. Alternatively, if used oils are combusted, metals in the flue gases can be released into the atmosphere unless they are captured by air pollution abatement equipment.

Source: Denton (2007).

Objectives and principles of the proposed reform

A product charge or recycling fee could address the diffuse pollution from this pollutant. The rate would depend on the product's toxicity to influence users' choices and disposal practices. If products are imported, a specific import duty could play this role.

Collection and recycling networks could be established to strengthen the proposed mechanism. This would contribute to the adequate disposal, re-use or recycling of used lubricants. Options were compared for the disposal of crankcase oils, and relevant alternatives considered (see Box 8.3).

The reform seeks primarily to introduce the polluter pays principle to some extent for diffuse pollution through a tax or fee that is passed onto end users. Proceeds from the fee can in turn contribute to sound management and safe disposal (or re-use or recycling) of the products targeted.

Box 8.3. **Deposit-refund system**

With a "deposit-refund mechanism", the product tax or import duty is refunded in exchange for returning the polluting product (e.g. waste lubricants) to a depot for safe storage and disposal. Disposal could include recycling and re-use as a fuel, such as using lubricants to generate heat in municipal boilers. However, there is no direct link between those who pay the tax or fee (consumers) and the potential refund that could be collected by garages, mechanics, car dealers, etc. In this case, the principle is limited to a buy-back scheme; full implementation of the deposit-refund system would require a new market for waste oil re-use, recycling and regeneration.

Source: (OECD, 2013) and authors' own findings.

Reform scenarios: Pesticides

For pesticides, the proposed reform scenarios are as follows:

- **Scenario I**: Introduction of taxation targeting the most hazardous pesticides
- **Scenario II**: Increase of fiscal incentives to favour alternative pest management control strategies.

Table 8.5. **Reform scenarios: Pesticides**

	Current situation	Scenario I: Medium term	Scenario II: Long term
Objective	Current use contributes to diffuse pollution, although there is some level of public monitoring as these products are exclusively imported, and some improvements have occurred; past issues with larger toxic stockpiles (are not likely to recur.	Introduction of a specific import value-added tax (as there is no national production of pesticides). Following international best practice, the import duty rate should be based on the level of toxicity of the pesticide; this would encourage the uptake of less toxic products. This instrument is favoured given the low transaction costs associated with implementation (monitoring, registration, collection, etc.) compared to a system downstream of the pesticide supply chain.	Revision of import duties on pesticides to encourage lower use by farmers beyond switching from hazardous to less harmful products. Ban on import of hazardous products.
Rate	The current tax system exempts pesticides from VAT, hence favouring their use with the objective to promote agriculture development. However, it is not clear whether the agricultural development benefits outweigh the negative fiscal and environmental impacts.	Differentiated duty rates *ad valorem*, with the duty rate depending on the level of toxicity: • 20% for hazardous pesticides (WHO II type) • 12% (i.e. at the level of present VAT) for medium toxicity (WHO III type) • 5% for lower toxic types (WHO U types)	Revised differentiated rates: • 20% for medium toxicity (WHO III type) • 12% for lower toxic types (WHO U types)
Basis	n.a.	*Ad valorem*: the value of imported or domestic products of specific toxicity class.	
Revenue allocation	n.a.	Support pesticide users in improving their farming practices so as to stimulate the use of most effective and less hazardous chemicals, in optimal quantities.	
Coherence with existing legislation	In coherence with current tax law	It will be necessary to make modifications to the Tax Code.	

Source: Authors' own findings.

The revenue implications of the proposed scenarios are shown in Table 8.6.

Table 8.6. **Revenue implications of the developed scenarios: Pesticides**

Expected additional revenue (in mln. KGS)

	At present		Scenario I Medium term	Scenario II Long term
Source	Value of imported goods in 2011	Revenue in 2011	Expected revenue	Expected revenue
Hazardous pesticides	1.66	0	0.33	0**
Insecticides*	149.16	0	17.9	29.8
Fungicides*	48.05	0	5.7	9.6
Herbicides*	209.66	0	25.1	41.9
Disinfectants, etc.*	27.16	0	3.2	5.4
Total	435.68	0	52.4	86.8

* Excluding hazardous pesticides.

** Due to the proposed ban on hazardous pesticides.

Source: Authors' own estimates based on data from Tables 8.4 and 8.5 and proposed duty rates.

Expected impacts: Pesticides

The scenarios generate gradual results to favour alternative pest control strategies both in the medium term (by encouraging the uptake of less hazardous pesticides) and in the long term (by optimising pesticide use).

One key variable for assessing the impacts of both scenarios is the price elasticity of demand, reflecting the modification of farmers' practices in response to changes in the price of pesticides. If pesticide prices go up, will farmers reduce their use of pesticides, and by how much? A thorough assessment of this issue goes beyond the scope of this report; however, looking at past experiences, farmers are expected to be relatively insensitive to higher prices, as price elasticity for pesticides is low (Pearce and Koundouri, 2003).

Farmers are expected to over-use pesticides, as under-use is associated with potentially unacceptable variations in crop yields; therefore, the reduction in use is expected to be proportionally lower than the increase of the price of pesticides. Furthermore, the tax on pesticides will force farmers to find the right balance between effectiveness of use and cost of pesticides so as to maximise their net benefit (i.e. the market value of the incremental harvest minus the incremental cost of pesticides). One would expect the proportion of the harvest value spent by farmers on pesticides would not change significantly compared to current figures, despite the added tax.

Scenario I

This scenario aims to encourage farmers to switch to less hazardous products in their pest control strategies. Currently, pesticides are exempt from VAT. The proposed options introduce a price signal through an *ad valorem* import duty, with a 20% rate for WHO II type pesticides, higher than the present VAT level (12%); while a 12% rate is suggested for less hazardous pesticides of WHO III type and a 5% rate for the products with lower toxicity (WHO U types). This would avoid favouring hazardous pesticides over more innocuous alternatives; farmers will adjust their pest control strategy by taking into account the effectiveness and prices of the pesticides they use.

Scenario II

Measures under Scenario I are expected to be strengthened under this long-term strategy, which aims to reduce the use of pesticides per hectare, once all or most products used do not exceed a certain level of toxicity, following the ban of the most hazardous pesticides.[5]

With lower and relatively homogenous (all of type WHO III or lower) levels of toxicity, the focus is on optimising pesticide used in agriculture. This higher price of pesticides is expected to have some effect on profits, thereby internalising environmental externalities, but the actual reduction in use will depend on the price elasticity of pesticides.

Synthesis of impacts (Pesticides)

Under both scenarios, positive social and environmental impacts can be expected; thus, the implementation of both scenarios in sequence would likely have a positive outcome.

However, Scenario II introduces a non-economic instrument through the ban on the most hazardous pesticides. This change is not expected to be a major consequence as the economic instrument in the previous phase (Scenario I) would have gradually displaced its use.

The expected impacts of the proposed scenarios are summarised in Table 8.7.

Table 8.7. **Introduction of import duty/VAT for pesticides: Synthesis of the expected impacts of the scenarios for reform**

	Impact compared to current situation	Scenario I	Scenario II
Economic and fiscal impacts	Businesses*	0/-	0/-
	Innovation and research	0	0/+
	Consumers and households	0/-	0/-
	Public budget	+	+
	Water utilities and irrigation service providers	+/0	+/0
	Specific regions or sectors	-/0	-
	Overall impact	0	0/-
Social impacts	Vulnerable groups	0	0/-
	Participation	0	0
	Public health and safety	+	+
	Overall impact	0/+	0
Environmental impacts	Climate	0/+	+
	Water quantity	0/+	0/+
	Water quality	+	+
	Water resources	+	+
	Overall impact	+	+

*Here meaning mostly farmers and agri-business.

Source: Based on authors' own findings.

Table 8.8. **Reform scenarios: Lubricants and waste oils**

	Current situation	Medium term: Scenario I Introduction of taxation to raise awareness of this diffuse pollution issue	Long term: Scenario II Combine taxation and market forces to support the development of effective disposal
Objective	The actual quantity of lubricants is not fully monitored, but their increased use (linked to the growth in the number of motorised vehicle) contributes to diffuse pollution.	Introduction of a specific import duty (as there is no national production of lubricants). Low transaction costs (for monitoring, registration, collection, etc.) are associated with implementation compared to a system downstream of the lubricant supply chain.	Revision of the tax introduced under Scenario I to encourage the import of more easily regenerable lubricants.
Rate	No specific recycling or environmental fee is levied on these products.	*Ad quantum*, equivalent of KGS 3 750 (EUR 50) per tonne of lubricant imported.	Differentiated import duty *(To be translated into percentage of values of the volumes imported)*: *(i)* equivalent of KGS 5 625 (EUR 75/tonne) for conventional lubricants with costly regeneration processes or polluting incineration; *(ii)* equivalent of KGS 1 875 (EUR 24/tonne) for lubricants more suitable for regeneration or with relatively less polluting incineration processes.
Basis	n.a.	*Ad quantum:* based on the total amount of imported product (in tonnes).	*Ad valorem*: as a percentage of the lubricants' value.
Revenue allocation	n.a.	Additional revenue would be allocated to improve monitoring of sector trade; increase awareness of mechanics and related professionals responsible for engine maintenance; set up and monitor pilot collection and disposal schemes for lubricants; explore the feasibility of developing facilities for the regeneration of waste oils locally.	Additional revenue would support the development of an effective collection and reclaiming process throughout the country. This would range from disposal to incineration as fuel, but also oil regeneration. It would require co-operation between the specialised public agency and private operators (national or international, with regeneration expertise).
Coherence with existing legislation	In coherence with current tax law	Modifications to the Tax Code will be necessary. A project could be developed to earmark the additional revenue from import duties. A small agency specialised in the management of this specific waste product could be created, enabling the development of a cluster around the collection, incineration and regeneration of lubricants in the long term.	

Source: Based on authors' own assessments.

Support and accompanying measures (Pesticides)

A series of measures have been identified as prerequisites for the enabling environment for this reform package and to enhance its political acceptability:

Short-term measures *(for Scenario I)*

- Amendments to the Tax Code that remove pesticides from the list of products exempt from VAT.

Long-term measure *(for Scenario II)*

- **A ban on hazardous pesticides** through the list of pesticides and agricultural chemicals allowed for use in the Kyrgyz Republic (the list is regularly revised and published by the State Department of Chemicalisation and Protection of Plants of the Ministry of Agriculture, Water Resources and Processing Industry of the Kyrgyz Republic). It is valid for the next five years.

The revenue implications of the proposed scenarios are set out in Table 8.9:

Table 8.9. **Revenue implications of the developed scenarios**

Expected additional revenue (in mln. KGS)

	Scenario I – Medium term	Scenario II – Long term
Source	Expected revenue	Expected revenue
Medium estimate (based on number of registered vehicles in 2010)	29.0	n.a.
High estimate (based on estimated current number of vehicles)	61.2	n.a.
Maximum estimate (based on population)	218.9	n.a.

Note: **n.a.**: estimates are not available.

Source: Authors' own findings.

Expected impacts (lubricants and waste oils)

Scenario I

Under this scenario, an import duty would fund awareness-raising efforts about diffuse pollution, set up and monitor pilot collection and disposal schemes, and explore developing local facilities for regeneration of waste oils. The import duty *ad quantum* (set at the equivalent of EUR 50/tonne of new lubricant) is expected to generate about EUR 100 for each tonne of disposed waste oil. This is close to the waste oil management costs estimated elsewhere (BIOIS, 2010). These resources could go to a specialised agency (a public or non-profit organisation) with expertise in dealing with this type of waste to develop the sector for adequate waste oil collection, recycling and disposal.

Scenario II

In the long term, combine taxation and market activity to support development of an effective reclaiming process for lubricants and waste oils. As a follow up on Scenario I, this long-term option would combine both public interventions (with a specialised agency funded by the import duty revenue) and the commercialisation of waste oils and regenerated material sold for profit by private operators. Figure 8.1 provides an overview of what the structure could look like.

The contribution to the import duty is needed to bear the environmental costs associated with the activity. Such a system requires the prior successful development of the scheme outlined in Scenario I, and time to control for the important transactions costs associated with this solution, as well as the potential adaptation and evolution of waste oil regeneration technology.

Figure 8.1. **Potential long-term system allowing for effective management of waste oils**

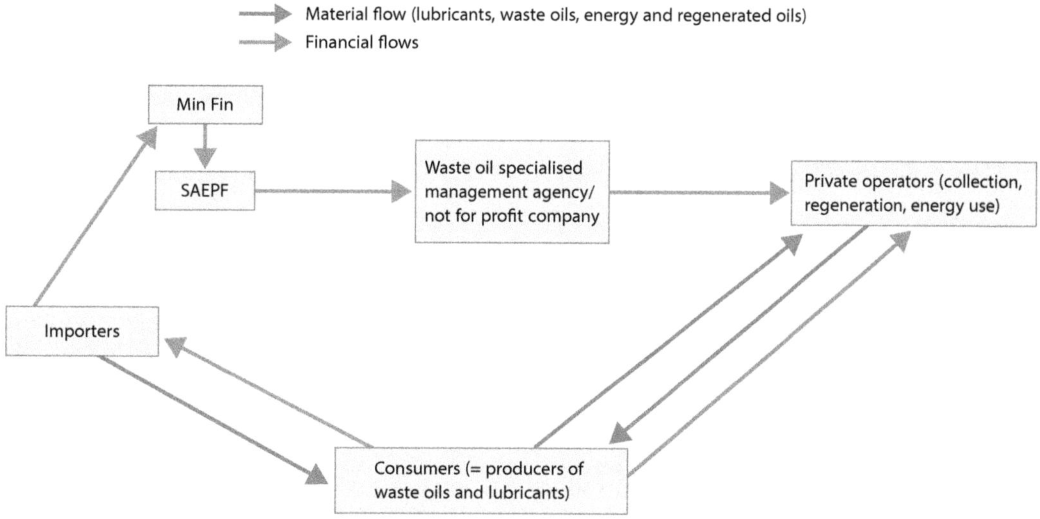

Note: **Min Fin**: Ministry of Finance of the Kyrgyz Republic. **SAEPF**: State Agency for Environmental Protection and Forestry under the Government of the Kyrgyz Republic.

Source: Authors' own proposal.

Table 8.10. **Introduction of import duty/VAT for lubricants: Synthesis of the expected impacts of the scenarios for reform**

	Impact compared to current situation	Scenario I	Scenario II
Economic and fiscal impacts	Businesses	0/-	0/-
	Innovation and research	0	+
	Consumers and households	0/-	0/-
	Public budget	+	+
	Water utilities and irrigation service providers	+/0	+/0
	Specific regions or sectors	-/0	-/0
	Overall impact	0/+	+
Social impacts	Vulnerable groups	0	0
	Participation	+	+
	Public health and safety	+	+
	Overall impact	+	+
Environmental impacts	Climate	0	0
	Water quantity	0	0
	Water quality	+	+
	Water resources	+	+
	Overall impact	+	+

Source: Based on authors' own calculations.

Synthesis of impacts (lubricants and waste oils)

Under both scenarios, positive social and environmental impacts can be expected; thus, the implementation of both scenarios in sequence would likely have a positive impact. A specific feasibility study would be required before the development of the waste oil regeneration sector in the long term.

The expected impacts of the proposed scenarios are summarised in Table 8.10.

Support and accompanying measures (lubricants and waste oils)

A series of measures have been identified as prerequisites for the enabling environment needed for this reform package and to enhance its political acceptability:

Short-term measures *(for Scenario I)*

- Amend the Tax Code to introduce an import duty on lubricants and use the resulting revenue to specifically fund the management of waste oils.
- Create a specialised public agency or non-profit organisation, under the authority of the SAEPF, to manage funds and develop a system to manage waste oils through regeneration into new oils and fuels.
- Develop links with ministries and public agencies responsible for transport and industries.

Long-term measures *(for Scenario II)*

- Revise rates of import duties according to degree of difficulty of managing waste. Two initial rates are proposed: a cheaper rate, corresponding to oils and lubricants that can be regenerated effectively or incinerated without major environmental impact, and a higher rate for those that cannot. The specialised agency would provide technical procedures.

Notes

1. Law of the Kyrgyz Republic: Technical Regulations "On the safety of drinking water" dated 30.05.2011, No. 3.
2. According to expert judgement, about 420-500 tonnes of pesticides are presently used (source: Division for plant protection and registration of pesticides of the State Department for Chemicalisation and Plant Protection, Ministry of Agriculture).
3. Includes automobiles, SUVs, vans, buses, commercial vehicles and freight motor road vehicles (excludes motorbikes and three-wheelers).
4. General Directorate of Traffic Safety. the Ministry of Internal Affairs of the Kyrgyz Republic.
5. However, this should be seen as a formality if Scenario I is effective in driving out remaining most hazardous pesticides.

References

BIOIS (2010), *Gestion de la filière de collecte et de valorisation des huiles usagées dans certains pays de l'Union européenne,* Report for the French Environment and Energy Management Agency (ADEME), Paris, www2.ademe.fr/servlet/getDoc?cid=96&m=3&id=69675&p1=00&p2=05&ref=17597.

Denton, J.E. (2007), *A review of the potential human and environmental health impacts of synthetic motor oils*, Office of Environmental Health Hazard Assessment, California Environmental Protection Agency, Sacramento, http://oehha.ca.gov/risk/pdf/SyntheticsFINAL-040607.pdf.

FAO (2014), *FAOSTAT – FAO Statistics Division*, Food and Agriculture Organization, Rome, http://faostat3.fao.org/faostat-gateway/go/to/search/PESTICIDES/E.

Kyrgyz Republic (2007), "The national plan for implementation of the Stockholm Convention", http://cbd.minjust.gov.kg/act/view/ru-ru/18596.

National Statistical Committee of the Kyrgyz Republic (2011), *Statistical Yearbook,* NCS, Bishkek.

OECD (2013), *Improving the Use of Economic Instruments for Water Resource Management in Kyrgyzstan: the Case of Lake Issyk-Kul Basin*, EAP Task Force, OECD Publishing, Paris, www.oecd.org/environment/outreach/Kyrgyzstan_Eis%20for%20WRM_2nd%20edition_ENG%20web.pdf.

OECD (2011a), *Strengthening financial planning and management for WSS in central government, municipalities and utilities of EECCA countries*, presentation on the national policy dialogue on financing strategy for urban and rural water supply and sanitation in the Kyrgyz Republic, Kiev, 24 April 2009, www.oecd.org/environment/outreach/42756430.pdf.

OECD (2011b), *Ten Years of Water Sector Reform in Eastern Europe, Caucasus and Central Asia*, OECD Publishing, Paris, http://dx.doi.org/10.1787/9789264118430-en.

Pearce, D. and P. Koundouri (2003), *Fertilizer and pesticide taxes for controlling non-point pollution, Agriculture and Rural Development (ARD)*, World Bank Group, Washington, DC.

Tauw (2009), *Interim Report, Obsolete Pesticides Technical Study in Kyrgyz Republic*, Report to the World Bank, Washington, DC., http://milieukontakt.net/en/wp-content/uploads/2009/12/R008-4640777BFF-sec-V01.pdf.

UNECE (2010), *Country Profiles on the Housing Sector: Kyrgyzstan*, United Nations Economic Commission for Europe, New York and Geneva, www.unece.org/fileadmin/DAM/hlm/documents/Publications/cp.kyrgyzstan.e.pdf.

UNECE (2009), *Environmental Performance Review: Kyrgyzstan, Second Review*, Environmental Performance Reviews Series No. 28, United Nations Economic Commission for Europe, New York and Geneva.

Chapter 9

Towards an Action Plan for reform of economic instruments for WRM in Kyrgyzstan

This chapter summarises recommended scenarios in the form of a draft Action Plan. For each instrument, the scenarios are seen as a continuum (an opportunity for gradual development) and as options that can be implemented either in sequence or in combination. The chapter stresses that implementation of the Action Plan provides a range of opportunities for Kyrgyzstan: it will help mobilise additional financial resources for water resource management through increased fiscal and tariff revenues, confer a greater degree of financial autonomy to operators of WSS and the state irrigation systems, and reduce the amount of public subsidies needed for operating and maintaining water infrastructure. The latter will free up significant public funding to support capital investment in water infrastructure, and to strengthen social support mechanisms targeting vulnerable social groups thus addressing possible social impacts of proposed reforms.

Introduction of surface water abstraction fees and water-body use charges

With regard to surface water abstraction fees, **gradual implementation of the reform is key**. The first step is to pilot the proposed approach in water-intensive sectors, i.e. in which water is a key input, but where it does not account for a majority of production costs, such as in the hydropower and mining sectors. The experience thus gained can then be applied to other water users. The development of this option should be harmonised across institutions to enable the following measures:

- linking surface water abstraction charges to a water abstraction permit system
- monitoring and enforcing surface water abstraction charges (although it entails additional costs)
- strengthening the existing state-funded social support system and targeting it at vulnerable groups (mainly linked to domestic water use and rural activity).

Reform of the level and structure of environmental pollution fees

Reforming environmental pollution fees brings a number of challenges that should be examined as a priority before reviewing the level of the fee, which had already been identified as too low. Among others, these include reviewing the calculation of the fees, and improved monitoring and enforcement to provide incentives for a more environment-friendly behaviour and generate adequate fiscal revenue. In this sense, Scenario I is clearly the first of a number of required sequential steps. Fees should be increased to give the instrument more teeth both financially (through increased fiscal revenue) and then as an incentive for pollution reduction. The impact of this increase in terms of revenue is difficult to calculate at this stage; a detailed analysis is required before engaging in reforms proposed under Scenarios IIb and IIa, particularly if Vodolkanals are no longer exempt from the pollution fee system.

Tariffs for irrigation water

The cost of irrigation in Kyrgyzstan is almost entirely subsidised, imposing an important burden on public finances due to the current low level of tariffs. A simple increase of existing tariffs to reach an adequate level of revenue remains an option. However, gradual implementation of a two-part tariff is preferable to ensure a more robust revenue base for managing the state irrigation network. Initially, the overall rate of the tariffs due by the WUAs could remain unchanged. Once the fixed part of the tariff is integrated into a differentiated land-tax system, it will bring accrued financial benefits due to higher collection efficiency; the collection rate for land tax is higher than for irrigation water tariffs.

Despite the apparent feasibility of tariff increases (linked to farmers' estimated willingness to pay), recent events in Kyrgyzstan have shown that increasing the price of any essential good or service is highly sensitive and can cause considerable social tension and unrest. The commitment to use a substantial part of the generated revenue for investments to maintain and rehabilitate the state irrigation system could significantly improve the acceptability of tariff increases.

The proposed reform of irrigation tariffs requires a careful sequencing of actions. In parallel with the reform, investments in the improvements of irrigation services, to be financed in part by the fixed component of the tariff, should be undertaken. Revenue from the variable component of the tariff would increase the financial sustainability of the irrigation network. Key to the success of the reform will be the institutional accountability and the allocation of financial revenue streams between the DWM&M and the water users' associations.

Reform of land tax in the Lake Issyk-Kul area

The Lake Issyk-Kul area has significant recreational and tourist value, for which it has been given the status of Biosphere Reserve. However, this factor was not taken into account when establishing the local land-tax system. The unique environmental and recreational benefits of the Lake Issyk-Kul area should be better reflected in this local tax.

The land tax coefficient for the area could be reviewed, and additional revenue earmarked for local water and municipal waste management, which is crucial to tourism in the area. The proposed adjustment of the coefficients would generate 30% additional revenue from land tax. Even without earmarking expected additional revenues, water resources management would benefit from a stronger fiscal position of the local and national governments (and respective public budgets) as they could allocate more funds for water sector priorities.

Although the impact will be felt locally, the changes in the land tax coefficient must be introduced at parliamentary level by amending the national Tax Code. This option should be considered as a mid- to long-term process by integrating this element into the local taxation system and integrating the environmental dimension into local public policy.

Reform of WSS tariff: Towards a two-part tariff

Adequate water pricing through WSS tariffs is a key element of the financing strategy for WSS services and is at the cornerstone of water resources management. Although there are examples of increasing volumetric tariffs to more adequate levels (e.g. in Bishkek), provincial towns lag behind in this respect (OECD, 2011a). A key feature of adequate pricing for WSS services, which is currently not in place in Kyrgyzstan, is the systematic installation of meters through a sound metering strategy; this should be developed both at the national and local levels, jointly with the municipalities and *Vodokanals* (water utilities).

Moreover, water supply and sanitation utilities can improve their financial sustainability by restructuring their pricing policy towards a two-part tariff (with a fixed and a variable component). This change can particularly benefit utilities facing a seasonal peak demand for water associated with tourism. Here the *Vodokanal* of Cholpon Ata is a good case study for two reasons: its location at the heart of the Lake Issyk-Kul tourism facilities, which attract 70% of all tourists travelling to, or within Kyrgyzstan; and current investments in improving WSS infrastructure through the Issyk-Kul Sustainable Development project funded by the Asian Development Bank.

The proposal includes the introduction of a two-part tariff for WSS services, and the extension of the number of connections to the sewerage network. The proposal has two implications: *(i)* the increase in the water supply tariff; and *(ii)* expansion of sanitation services, meaning that an increasing share of the population will be paying for a new service. In terms of affordability, the tariff increase is important in nominal terms over the period reviewed. The effect of offering a new service will need to be monitored, particularly for the poorest segment of the population.

As the pricing policy for WSS services is guided by the state, tariffs are subject to approval by the municipal council called *Kenesh,* in concurrence with the local representative of the state anti-monopoly service responsible for the regulation of prices and tariffs. Following the political instability in 2010, affordability concerns pushed local authorities to revert to lower volumetric tariffs, despite the need to increase them two-fold over 2009-25 to recover basic costs and provide adequate WSS services to all. This precedent highlights the need to analyse, on a case by case basis, the issues of water pricing and affordability to respond effectively to the challenges of WSS service provision. Table 9.1 presents a draft action plan based on the above considerations and on the recommendations in this report.

Product tax (including custom duty) on selected pollutants

The introduction of a specific import duty *ad valorem* on agricultural chemicals (as there is no national production of pesticides and other chemicals) should follow international best practice, i.e. import duty rates should reflect the level of toxicity of respective chemicals to encourage uptake of less toxic products. This instrument is favoured given the low transaction costs associated with implementation (costs monitoring, registration, collection, etc.) compared with a system downstream of the pesticide supply chain. In a mid-term perspective, impose ban on import (or eventual local production) of most hazardous agricultural chemicals.

Farmers should be compensated for the increased cost of agricultural chemicals through more cost-effective forms of state support to agriculture, including through: *(i)* developing rural infrastructure (roads, WSS systems etc.) and the network of crop storage facilities; *(ii)* supporting farmers, WUAs and co-operatives of farmers to introduce more efficient irrigation techniques, etc.

A collection and recycling network should complement the levy on lubricants to help with the adequate disposal, re-use or recycling of used lubricants. Key elements of such a system could be pilot tested in one region, e.g. Issyk-Kul Oblast.

Table 9.1. **Draft Action Plan for the reform of economic instrument for water resources management**

Instrument	Action proposed	Responsible institution*	Timeframe	Resource implications (incremental costs etc.)	Success criteria; Performance indicators (PIs)	Performance monitoring and evaluation	Completion date**
			A. Short-term actions (to be implemented in year 1)				
Surface water abstraction fees and water-use permits	Re-instatement of water abstraction and water-use permits by amending existing legislation.	DWM&M	1 year	Cost of mobilising expert and legal team (may require external assistance).	Permit issuance; **PIs**: number of permits issued; amount of water licensed for abstraction.	Annual report (green paper) presented to the Kyrgyz government and Parliament.	Jan. 2016
Surface water abstraction fees	Prepare and submit to the Parliament draft amendments to the Water Code and other water-related legislation (changes and amendments needed to the legislation and sub-law regulation on irrigation services and WSS).	DWM&M	9 months	Cost of mobilising expert and legal team*** (may require external assistance).	Law adopted by the Parliament (*Jogorku Kenesh*) and the charge is introduced.	Annual report (green paper) presented to the Kyrgyz government and Parliament.	Dec. 2015
Surface water abstraction fees	Prepare a draft sub-law regulation on surface water abstraction charges and submit it for approval to government. The regulation should set rules, procedures and responsibilities for calculating and paying the charges, as well as establish sanctions for violations.	DWM&M	1 year	Cost of mobilising expert and legal team (may require external assistance).	Sub-law regulation approved by the Kyrgyz government; **PIs**: total water abstraction charge revenue (on an accrual basis), collection efficiency; number of violations identified.	Annual report (green paper) presented to the Kyrgyz government and Parliament.	Dec. 2015
Irrigation tariff	Introduce legislative proposal for a two-part tariff for irrigation.	DWM&M	1 year	Cost of mobilising expert and legal team (may require external assistance).	Sub-law regulation approved by the Kyrgyz government and two-part tariffs used; **PIs**: cost recovery ratio of the two-part tariff (of fixed and O&M costs)	Annual report on established performance indicators.	2017 and beyond
WSS tariffs	Draft proposal for tariff changes for the period 2015-25 (including two-part tariffs); consult on the draft with public and other stakeholders.	Cholpon Ata Vodokanal, Municipality of Cholpon Ata	1 year	Cost of mobilising expert and legal team, including financial expertise (may require external assistance).	Programme of defined increase in tariffs and change in tariff structure approved by public authorities; proposals for reform drafted internally by the Vodokanals; **PI**: recovery of O&M costs by WSS tariffs.	Annual reports by Vodokanals on key performance indicators (including tariff levels; revenue, collection efficiency and arrears by consumer category, etc.)	Dec. 2015

Table 9.1. **Draft Action Plan for the reform of economic instrument for water resources management** *(continued)*

Instrument	Action proposed	Responsible institution*	Timeframe	Resource implications (incremental costs etc.)	Success criteria; Performance indicators (PIs)	Performance monitoring and evaluation	Completion date**
A. Short-term actions (to be implemented in year 1) – Continued							
Land tax	Amendments to the legislation to revise basic land-tax use rates for settlements (with a specific rate for tourism and recreational infrastructure) and to differentiate the rates depending on the availability of water infrastructure (WSS, storm water, flood, mud flow and groundwater flooding protection) in the Issyk-Kul Biosphere reserve area.	Ministry of Finance, Municipalities of Issyk-Kul area	1 year	Cost of mobilising expert and legal team (may require external assistance).	Revised land-tax rates (Art. 337, 338 and 339) **PI:** additional land tax revenue from the land plots in Issyk-Kul area used by tourism and recreation businesses	Annual report on established performance indicators	Dec. 2015
Import duty on pesticides	Legislative proposal for introduction of import duty on pesticides, according to their toxicity and/or to remove pesticides from the list of products exempt from VAT.	Ministry of Agriculture and Melioration of the Kyrgyz Republic SAEPF, Ministry of Economy	1 year	Cost of mobilising legal and financial teams (may require external assistance).	Sub-law regulation approved by the Kyrgyz government; **PIs:** creation of import duty on pesticides	Annual report by Customs	2016 and beyond
B. Mid-term actions (to be implemented between year 1 and year 5)							
Water abstraction and pollution fees	Submit proposal to earmark a significant proportion of total revenue from water abstraction and pollution fees for water-related projects and initiatives.	DWM&M Dept. of WSS SAEPF; Ministry of Finance Ministry of Economy	1-3 years	Cost of internal government process.	The creation of clear earmarking mechanism **PIs:** *(i)* total water abstraction and pollution fees (on an accrual basis), *(ii)* collection efficiency, *(iii)* share of revenue spent on water project; and *(iv)* number of violations identified and penalties levied.	Annual report on established performance indicators.	2017
Pollution fees/ abstraction fees	Launch a diagnostic of the industrial sector in terms of reducing pollution and improving resource efficiency (this should not be limited to water, but also to energy and other key resource inputs).	Ministry of Economy, DWM&M SAEPF Industry representatives, Energy-related administrative bodies	1-3 years	Mobilise expertise.	An assessment of the industrial sector's pollution levels and resource intensity.	Annual report on established performance indicators.	2017
Pollution fees	Develop a proposal for extending access to NFEP funding (and other related mechanisms) to the private sector.	Ministry of Finance, SAE&F	1-3 years	Mobilise expertise.	NFEP reformed; Private sector can apply for support for their pollution abatement initiatives.		2017

Table 9.1. **Draft Action Plan for the reform of economic instrument for water resources management** *(continued)*

Instrument	Action proposed	Responsible institution*	Timeframe	Resource implications (incremental costs etc.)	Success criteria; Performance indicators (PIs)	Performance monitoring and evaluation	Completion date**
B. Mid-term actions (to be implemented between year 1 and year 5) *– Continued*							
Irrigation tariff	Link agriculture improvement programmes focusing on more efficient practices (i.e. energy, water, inputs in general) to the introduction of irrigation tariffs.	Ministry of Agriculture, Ministry of Economy DWM&M	1-5 years	Efforts in co-ordinating agriculture and rural development programmes with water management initiatives to promote the uptake of more efficient water technologies.	Increased water efficiency in agriculture **PIs:** water intensity of key agri-products; water use by crop.	Introduce a section into government reports on agriculture and rural development, presenting agreed water use efficiency indicators (time series).	2020
Irrigation tariff	Provide targeted support to the most vulnerable quintile of farmers.	Ministry of Economy, Ministry of Finance, Ministry of Agriculture. Ministry of Social Development *(optional)*	1-5 years (Continuous)	*(i)* transaction costs associated with identifying and targeting lowest income quintile of farmers; *(ii)* cost of financial support.	Most vulnerable quintile of farmers is identified and supported. **PIs:** number of vulnerable farmers getting support and its value.	Annual report on established performance indicators.	2017 and beyond
WSS tariffs	Strengthen the capacity of financial officers and accountants of Cholpon Ata *Vodokanal* (and that of all Vodokanals).	Dept. of WSS, Association of Vodokanals *(optional)*	1-3 years	Training and follow up.	All financial officers and accountants are able to prepare a plan for increasing and restructuring tariffs, to be submitted to the public authorities in charge.		2017
WSS tariffs	Prioritise the installation of meters all over the country.	Vodokanals, Association of Vodokanals, local public authorities	1-5 years	• Develop a metering strategy • Purchase and install meters • Build human capacity to carry out the installation, operation and maintenance of meters, including meter reading.	95+% of houses and apartment buildings using piped water have water meters and pay against meter readings; **PIs:** share of billing based on actual (metered) water consumption in lcd; non-revenue water (l/conn/day).	Annual report of key performance indicators (by Vodokanals)	2020

Table 9.1. **Draft Action Plan for the reform of economic instrument for water resources management** *(continued)*

Instrument	Action proposed	Responsible institution*	Timeframe	Resource implications (incremental costs etc.)	Success criteria; Performance indicators (PIs)	Performance monitoring and evaluation	Completion date**
***B. Mid-term actions (to be implemented between year 1 and year 5)** – Continued*							
WSS tariffs	If affordability of water supply services remains a barrier to service for vulnerable groups, additional support could be provided by limiting the tariff to be paid for both water supply and sanitation services to the fixed part of the tariff – up to a certain level of consumption, adequately monitored through metering. This measure requires the installation of meters and the development of a strategy to reduce non-revenue water (i.e. leaks and non-collected bills).	Pilot established (e.g. municipality of Cholpon Ata).	1-5 years, as tariffs are reviewed	Technical support and the mobilisation of the municipal authorities.	Most vulnerable quintile of households are identified, have access to piped water supply and contribute in a limited way to the service. **PIs:** the number of vulnerable households getting support and its value.	Annual report on performance (by *Vodokanal*)	2020
WSS tariffs	Subsidise the connection to the network ("last mile") for all households. User cost can then be transferred to households, at least partially, given the existence of willingness to pay for water supply.	Pilot established (e.g. municipality of Cholpon Ata)	1-5 years	Mobilise technical expertise. Mobilise national and international funding.	Investment plan updated and fully subsidised. **PI:** number of new connections and the amount of subsidy.		2020
Import duty on lubricants and oils	Amendments to the legislation to revise the Tax Code so as to introduce an import duty on lubricants and use funding to manage waste oils.	SAEPF, MinFin	1-3 years	Mobilise technical expertise, Mobilise national and international funding.	Special import duty on lubricants for recycling and regeneration created.	New import duty in place.	2017
B. Mid-term actions (to be implemented between year 1 and year 5) – Continued							
Import duty on lubricants and oils	Create a specialised public agency or non-profit organisation, under the authority of the SAEPF, to manage funds and be responsible for the management and regeneration of waste oils.	SAEPF	1-3 years	Mobilise technical expertise. Mobilise national and international funding.	Specialised waste oil agency/non-profit organisation created.	Registration of agency/ company and first annual report of activities.	2017

Table 9.1. **Draft Action Plan for the reform of economic instrument for water resources management** *(continued)*

Instrument	Action proposed	Responsible institution*	Timeframe	Resource implications (incremental costs etc.)	Success criteria; Performance indicators (PIs)	Performance monitoring and evaluation	Completion date**
B. Enabling environment. Medium-term supporting and accompanying measures							
All instruments	A more detailed assessment of accompanying and support measures (for vulnerable groups and relevant economic sectors).	Ministries, respective International agencies	1-2 years	Technical support and the mobilisation of management at various levels (from municipal and water user associations to ministries); need to ensure coherence of such measures with the national development strategy and sector policies.	The actual costs and benefits of each measure is reviewed to ensure a cost-effective implementation of the economic instrument.	Assessment of the implementation of reformed/new economic instruments.	2017
All instruments	Information/public awareness campaigns, informing about the "true" costs of water management so that better-informed citizens could contribute to it.	DWM&M, Ministry of Education	1-3 years	Develop a communication campaign (maybe starting on a special day like *Earth Day* or *World Water Day* or another Kyrgyzstan significant date).	Percentage of the population reached by communication.	Evaluation report on the campaign.	Jan. 2017
C. Long-term actions (5+ years)							
Irrigation tariff	Develop regulatory mechanism to orient water savings from agricultural use to the aquifers or environment in general. Ensure minimum environmental flows.	SAEPF, DWM&M	5-10 years	Cost of mobilising expert and legal team (may require external assistance).	Stabilise water use levels; **PIs** – to be elaborated (*option*: minimal environmental flow set in percentage of multi-annual average run-off).	Annual report on established performance indicators.	2025
Irrigation tariff	Continue to support the uptake of water-efficient technology in co-ordination with larger rural development programmes	SAEPF, DWM&M	5-10 years	Efforts in co-ordinating agriculture and rural development programmes with water management initiatives to promote uptake of more efficient water technologies.	Increase water efficiency in agriculture **PI:** water intensity of agri-products (per tonne of produce).	Assessment report on last 10 years of promoting water-efficient technologies in agriculture.	2025
Pollution fees	Targeted support programme (financing and guidance) for the improvement of processes to support innovation in pollution abatement and resource intensity reduction.	Ministry of Economy, DWM&M, SAEPF, industry representatives, energy-related administrative bodies.	5-10 years	Mobilise expertise, national and international funding.	Pollution levels have been reduced, along with resource intensity of individual production processes. **PI**: resource intensity of specific production processes.	Annual report on established performance indicators.	2025

Table 9.1. **Draft Action Plan for the reform of economic instrument for water resources management** *(continued)*

Instrument	Action proposed	Responsible institution*	Timeframe	Resource implications (incremental costs etc.)	Success criteria; Performance indicators (PIs)	Performance monitoring and evaluation	Completion date**
C. Long-term actions (5+ years) – Continued							
Land tax	Amendments to the legislation and revision of basic land-tax use rates (agriculture, gardens and settlements) and differentiating the rates depending on availability of water infrastructure (WSS, storm water, flood, mud flow and groundwater flooding protection) in Kyrgyzstan.	Municipalities of Issyk-Kul Oblast, Ministry of Finance.	5-10 years	Mobilise expert and legal team (may require external assistance).	Revised land-tax rates (Art. 337, 338 and 339) **PI:** additional land tax revenue stream.	Annual report on established performance indicators.	2025
Import duty on pesticides	Ban on hazardous pesticides, through the list of pesticides and agricultural chemicals allowed for use in the Kyrgyz Republic (currently under review).	Department of Chemicalisation and Protection of Plants at the Ministry of Agriculture and Melioration	5-10 years	No incremental cost (routine work of line ministries and custom service).	Revised list of authorised products.	The list is regularly published by the department and is valid for the next 5-year term.	2020 onwards
Import duty on lubricants and oils	Integrate waste management into industrial and trading strategy of the country. Develop links with ministries and public agencies responsible for industrial development.	SAEPF	1-3 years (and beyond)	No incremental cost (routine work of line ministries and custom service).	Oil waste management and regeneration is considered as a sector positively contributing to the economy. **PI**: amount of waste oil regenerated.	Annual report on the turnover of sector.	2017 and beyond
Import duty on lubricants and oils	Revision of rates of import duty according to degree of difficulty of managing waste. A cheaper rate, corresponding to oils and lubricants that can be regenerated or incinerated effectively, and a higher rate for those that cannot. Technical procedures should be provided by the specialised agency.	Ministry of Finance and specialised agency on oil management under the SAEPF	5-10 years	Internal process in co-ordination with oil recyclers and regenerators.	Rates of import duty are adapted. **PI:** new import duty rates.	Annual report by the custom service.	2025 and beyond

* Where relevant, the name of the leading institution is underlined.

** Assuming 1 January 2015 as start date.

*** The expert and legal team may include environmentalists, economists, financial (public finance) and legal experts.

Note: A question mark "?" indicates an option, not an obligation.

Source: Based on authors' own findings.

References

BIOIS (2010), *Gestion de la filière de collecte et de valorisation des huiles usagées dans certains pays de l'Union européenne,* Report for the French Environment and Energy Management Agency (ADEME), Paris, www2.ademe.fr/servlet/getDoc?cid=96&m=3&id=69675&p1=00&p2=05&ref=17597.

Denton, J.E. (2007), "*A review of the potential human and environmental health impacts of synthetic motor oils*", Office of Environmental Health Hazard Assessment, California Environmental Protection Agency, Sacramento, http://oehha.ca.gov/risk/pdf/SyntheticsFINAL-040607.pdf.

EC (2009), "*Impact assessment guidelines*", 15 January 2009, SEC(2009)92, European Commission, Brussels.

Egenhofer, C., et al. (2012), "*Which economic model for a water-efficient Europe?*" *CEPS Task Force Report*, 27 November 2012, Centre for European Policy Studies, Brussels.

EPA (2007), "*Assessing health risks from pesticides*", United States Environmental Protection Agency, Washington, DC., www.epa.gov/pesticides/factsheets/riskassess.htm.

FAO (2014), *FAOSTAT – FAO Statistics Division*, Food and Agriculture Organization, Rome, http://faostat3.fao.org/faostat-gateway/go/to/search/PESTICIDES/E.

Kyrgyz Republic (2011), *Law of the Kyrgyz Republic from 30 May 2011 of No. 34 Technical regulation: On the safety of drinking water.*

Kyrgyz Republic (2007), *The national plan for implementation of the Stockholm Convention*, http://cbd.minjust.gov.kg/act/view/ru-ru/18596.

National Statistical Committee of the Kyrgyz Republic (2013), *Statistical Yearbook, Bishkek.*

Nippon Koei Co. Ltd, and RAM Engineering Associates (2009a), *City level infrastructure plan (CLIP), Cholpon Ata, Issyk-Kul sustainable development project*, Kyrgyz Republic, *Report ADB TA NO. 7228 KGZ*, Volume 1, Bishkek.

Nippon Koei Co. Ltd, and RAM Engineering Associates (2009b), *Social assessment, Cholpon Ata, Issyk-Kul sustainable development project*, Kyrgyz Republic, *Report ADB TA NO. 7228 KGZ,* Volume 8, Bishkek.

OECD (2013), *Improving the Use of Economic Instruments for Water Resource Management in Kyrgyzstan: the Case of Lake Issyk-Kul Basin*, EAP Task Force, OECD Publishing, Paris, www.oecd.org/environment/outreach/Kyrgyzstan_Eis%20for%20WRM_2nd%20edition_ENG%20web.pdf.

OECD (2011a), *Strengthening financial planning and management for WSS in central government, municipalities and utilities of EECCA countries*, presentation on the national policy dialogue on financing strategy for urban and rural water supply and sanitation in the Kyrgyz Republic, Kiev, 24 April 2009, www.oecd.org/environment/outreach/42756430.pdf.

OECD (2011b), *Ten Years of Water Sector Reform in Eastern Europe, Caucasus and Central Asia*, OECD Publishing, Paris, http://dx.doc.org/10.1787/9789264118430-en.

Pearce, D. and P. Koundouri (2003), *Fertilizer and pesticide taxes for controlling non-point pollution, Agriculture and Rural Development (ARD)*, World Bank Group, Washington, DC.

Polimeni, J., et al. (2008), *The Jevons Paradox and the Myth of Resource Efficiency Improvements*. Earthscan, London.

SIAR (2013), *Survey of tourism market in Kyrgyzstan. Report to the USAID Local Development Program*, Social and Marketing Research Centre, Baku City.

Smets, H. (2008), *De l'eau potable à un prix abordable: La pratique des États,* Académie de l'eau, Nanterre.

Tauw (2009), *Interim Report, Obsolete Pesticides Technical Study in Kyrgyz Republic*, Report to the World Bank, Washington, DC., http://milieukontakt.net/en/wp-content/uploads/2009/12/R008-4640777BFF-sec-V01.pdf.

UNECE (2010), *Country Profiles on the Housing Sector: Kyrgyzstan*, United Nations Economic Commission for Europe, New York and Geneva, www.unece.org/fileadmin/DAM/hlm/documents/Publications/cp.kyrgyzstan.e.pdf.

UNECE (2009), *Environmental Performance Review: Kyrgyzstan, Second Review*, Environmental Performance Reviews Series No. 28, United Nations Economic Commission for Europe, New York and Geneva.

UNECE (2000), *Environmental Performance Review: Kyrgyzstan,* Environmental Performance Reviews Series No. 9, United Nations Economic Commission for Europe, New York and Geneva.

Annex A

List of government officials interviewed in the context of this project

To develop an updated understanding of the current challenges, and gather data for the development of the scenarios for reform and their possible impacts, the following government officials and specialists were contacted and interviewed between July 2013 – April 2014:

- Mr Abdybai Djailoobaev, Deputy Director General of Department of Water Management and Melioration, Ministry of Agriculture and Melioration; and Chairman of the NPD
- Mr Abdykalyk Rustamov – Deputy Director, Agency for Environmental Protection and Forestry
- Ms Djyparkul Bekkulova – Head of Environmental Strategy and Policy Department, State Agency for Environmental Protection and Forestry
- Mr Keneshbek Djumabekov, Head of Ecological Assessment and Nature Management Department, State Agency for Environmental Protection and Forestry
- Ms Liubov Ten, Advisor to Minister, Ministry of Economy and Anti-monopoly Policy
- Ms Galina Klimakova, Department of Financing of Agricultural Sector, Ministry of Finance
- Ms Ekaterina Sakhvaeva, Head of Informational and Analytical Centre, Department of Water Management and Melioration, Ministry of Agriculture and Melioration
- Ms Shairgul Orozbakieva, Department of Water Supply and Wastewater Development, State Agency for Construction and Communal Utilities Development
- Ms Kadoeva Jamal, Chief Specialist at Environmental Strategy and Policy Department, State Agency for Environmental Protection and Forestry
- Mr Almaz Alakunov, Head of Division for Plant Protection and Registration of Pesticides of the State Department for Chemicalisation and Plant Protection of the Ministry of Agriculture and Melioration
- Prof. Ainash A. Sharshenova, Head of the Department for Environmental Health, Scientific and Production Centre for Preventive Medicine (SPCPM) of the Ministry of Health of the Kyrgyz Republic
- Mr Erkinbek Kojoev, Coordinator of Institutional Development, World Bank-funded "Second On-Farm Irrigation Project".

Annex B

Expert workshop (Bishkek, 18 March 2014)

In the framework of the project, an expert meeting was organised to submit various options and scenarios to a group of experts and stakeholders and discuss their relevance, strengths and weaknesses. Following a presentation of the methodology, proposed reforms of selected instruments were discussed.[1] The discussions mainly focused on *(i)* general methodological/presentation aspects; *(ii)* irrigation tariffs; *(iii)* environmental fees; and *(iv)* the Action Plan. Recommendations by experts participating in the meeting were as follows:

1. Methodology
   - Clearly explain the focus on the medium term (up to 5-7 years) by referring to the National Sustainable Development Strategy timeline; and indicate that longer-term options are analysed for reference.
   - Clarify the disbursement systems, beyond the simple concept of earmarking, where relevant.
2. Reform of environmental pollution fees
   - Include possibility of private beneficiaries from the Republican Fund.
   - Envisage targeted support for pollution abatement technologies for the long-term (there are recent precedents with subsidies for private investment in pollution abatement and control through the "Village II" project on agriculture funded by commercial bank loans and Ministry of Finance subsidies.
   - Include benchmarking from neighbouring countries on environmental pollution fees, if possible.
3. Reform of irrigation tariffs
   - Make the point that we should avoid subsidising water use, but rather provide incentives for water saving and more efficient water uses.
   - Target subsidies on intra-farming solutions, instead of public network solutions.
   - Indicate cost of water/total production cost ratio in agriculture.
   - Recognise that WUAs fully support a two-part tariff approach, but increased tariffs for water should not be a reason to withdraw support from agriculture. Increases should be on top of current subsidies.
   - Include an additional Scenario *0b* where estimates are made for an improved collection rate of the current fee to 95%, instead of the current 50%.

4. Action Plan (AP):
   - Make better monitoring a priority, as current reports seem to suggest that water pollution is not such a problem.
   - Address remaining gaps in legislation as a priority over increasing tariffs.

Agenda

Time	Session	Interventions	Speakers
14:00	**Welcome, objectives, agenda, tour de table**		Mr Isabekov (DWR&M)
14:05	**National context**	The NPD process in Kyrgyzstan, recent reform of economic instruments for water management	Mr Isabekov (DWR&M) *
14:20	**Introduction of the study and its methods**	Context and methodology	Mr Garzón Delvaux (ACTeon)
14:40	**The results of the study**	Detail presentation of each instrument, followed by specific discussion on implementation	Mr Garzón Delvaux (ACTeon)/ All participants Facilitation: Mr Garzón Delvaux (ACTeon)
15:40	**Coffee break**		
15:50	**Towards an Action Plan**	Key elements of the proposed Action Plan	Mr Garzón Delvaux (ACTeon)
16:15	**The Action Plan within the larger picture**	Collective review of the Action Plan	All participants Facilitation: Mr Isabekov (DWR&M)
17:15	**Closing session**	Synthesis of the workshop	Mr Garzón Delvaux (ACTeon)
17:30		*Tour de table*: Last words and ideas from each participant Concluding remarks of chairman	All participants Facilitation: Mr Isabekov (DWR&M)
17:45	**End of the workshop**		

* Mr Isabekov could not attend because of a last minute official meeting, so there was no major presentation on the current context; discussions focused on the study.

Participants

#	РУССКИЙ	ENGLISH	CONTACTS
1	**Климакова Галина** Николаевна Главный специалист отдела финансирования АПК, природо-пользования и ЧС Министерства финансов Кыргызской Республики	**Klimakova Galina** Chief Specialist, Ministry of Finance of the Kyrgyz Republic	T: +996 312 660504 F: +996312 664208 E: g.klimakova@minfin.kg
2	**Соловьева Татьяна** Викторовна Главный специалист отдела гидрологии Агентства по гидрометеорологии при МЧС	**Soloviova Tatiana** Chief Specialist of the Hydrology Department, Kyrgyzhydromet	T: +996 312 316 294 E: meteo@meteo.ktnet.kg
3	**Байдакова Наталья** Сергеевна Заместитель начальника Управления экологической стратегии, политики и пресс – службы Государственного агентства охраны окружающей среды и лесного озяйства при Правительстве Кыргызской Республики	**Baidakova Natalia** Deputy head of the Department of Ecological Strategy, Policy and Mass Media, State Agency on Environment Protection and Forestry under the Government of the Kyrgyz Republic (SAEPF)	T: +996 312 549 487 E: ecokg@aknet.kg

#	РУССКИЙ	ENGLISH	CONTACTS
4	**Раимкулова А.К.** Главный специалист Управления государственной экологической экспертизы и природопользования Госагентства охраны окружающей среды и лесного хозяйства	**Raiymkulova A. K.** Senior Specialist of State Ecological Expertise Management, State Agency on Environment Protection and Forestry under the Government of the Kyrgyz Republic (SAEPF)	+996 312 352727 E: raimkulova.asel@mail.ru
5	**Кожоев Эркин** Республиканский Союз АВП Кыргызстана	**Kozoev Erkin** AWU Union of the Kyrgyz Republic	+996 312 545691 E: wua.union.kg@gmail.com
6	**Валентини Кирилл** Консультант	**Valentini Kirill** Consultant	T. +996 312 381 552 M: +996 550 638 584 E: kvalentini@mail.ru
7	**Педро Андрес Гарсон Д.** Консультант Актеон (ACTeon)	**Pedro Andrés Garzón D.** Consultant ACTeon	E: a.garzon@acteon-environment.eu
8	**Неронова Таисия** Консультант	**Neronova Taisia** Consultant	E: neronova@rambler.ru
9	**Жунусбаев Калыйбек** Консультант	**Zhunusbaev Kalyibek** Consultant	E: chabyt@gmail.com
10	**Джиенбекова Азиза** Ассистент проекта	**Jienbekova Aziza** Project Assistant	E: oecdkgfs@gmail.com

Note

1. But suggestions for a tax/import duty on products contributing to diffuse pollution were not yet developed at that time.

Annex C

Details of the assessment: Tables for all instruments

Note: The source of all tables in Annex C: authors' own assessment.

Table C.1. **Establishment of a water component in existing land-tax rates in the vicinity of Lake Issyk-Kul: Impact assessment of the proposed scenarios**

ECONOMIC AND FISCAL IMPACTS			
Impacts on	Key questions	Scenario I	Scenario II (land tax rate increase by 30%)
		Impact assessment	
Business	Will the tax increase pose an additional burden on local SMEs?	The great majority of the 139 hotels and 370 tourism-related businesses registered in the Issyk-Kul area will have to contribute, but this cost can be passed onto tourists so that they also actively contribute to water and land management.	Not really, as the tax is still marginal and the additional burden is expected to be passed onto consumers.
Innovation and research	Will higher revenue for the sector correspond to higher investments in innovation and research?	Unlikely.	Since the instrument will generate additional revenue, the earmarked money can be used to fund some innovative projects.
	Does it promote greater productivity and resource efficiency?	In some cases, the targeted tax could be an incentive for some establishments to adopt best practices.	The instrument itself does not directly promote greater productivity or resources efficiency, though some pilot projects might be targeted towards that, in the territories where resource scarcity issues exist.
Consumers and households	Does the instrument have budgetary consequences for individual users and households?	Not generally. Only tourists are affected if the hotels transfer costs onto them.	All users are affected and will have to contribute more to water and land management in the region this way.
Public budget	Does the instrument have budgetary consequences for public authorities at different levels of government?	A small increase in revenue can be expected.	In the proposed scenario for reform, the extra revenue (30%) generated by the reform are earmarked and used by the oblast for water management and protection of aquatic ecosystems. Some minor administrative costs will occur linked to earmarking. However, these costs are likely to be much lower than increased revenue.
Water utilities and irrigation service providers	How does the instrument financially affect water service companies and organisations?	Some additional revenue are expected, but they are only marginal.	New revenue streams, earmarked or partially earmarked to water management are expected to contribute to raise standards of water quality.
Specific sectors	Would the tax increase have a significant impact on specific sectors?	This instrument is specifically targeting the tourism sector.	Land tax changes are expected to have an impact on all sectors, but agriculture is likely to be affected the most.

Table C.1. **Establishment of a water component in existing land-tax rates in the vicinity of Lake Issyk-Kul: Impact assessment of the proposed scenarios** *(continued)*

SOCIAL IMPACTS			
Impacts on	Key questions	Scenario I	Scenario II
		Impact assessment	
Vulnerable groups	Is the tax increase affordable on average?	No, vulnerable groups are expected to be affected the most.	According to the NSC (2013) for the year 2012, all expenditure for taxes and fees represented 6% of income per capita in average for the Issyk-Kul Oblast (Urban average was 7.8% and rural 5.4%). A 30% increase will still be affordable for the average household. The land tax to household income ratio is then expected to increase by up to 2%.
	Is the tax increase affordable for low-income groups?	Low-income groups are not likely to be affected as they are less likely to have tourism-related expenditure.	Although there is no specific threshold for the tax/income ratio for this group, a 30% increase could create affordability problems for some households in the low-income group. The land tax is expected to have a larger impact on the poor as many of them are rural, and depend more on cash subsistence income (mainly based on land) than on regular cash income and often have only land as a safety net. However, the extremely poor may be proportionally less affected than the poor as they only have very limited access to land.* Moreover, the percentage of tax-related expenditure is lower in rural than in urban areas: tax/income burden in urban areas averages 7.8% whereas in rural it is 5.4% (NSC, 2013).
Participation	Does the instrument make the public more aware of issues related to sustainable water use and ecosystem protection?	This is likely to be the case if the scheme offers a tax relief for water users showing good practice; and this can be in turn marketed by operators to tourists.	Since the extra revenue (30%) generated by the reform will be used by the local governments for water management and protection of aquatic ecosystem, naturally public awareness on sustainable water use and ecosystem protection will be enhanced.
Public health and safety	Does the instrument increase or decrease the likelihood of health risks due to substances harmful to the natural environment?	Less untreated discharges are expected, although the overall impacts may not be significant.	Due to the implementation of environmental projects, which will improve the water quality and overall environmental quality, the instrument will decrease the likelihood of health risks in the Issyk-Kul area.

*Inspired from NIPPON KOEI (2009).

Table C.1. **Establishment of a water component in existing land-tax rates in the vicinity of Lake Issyk-Kul: Impact assessment of the proposed scenarios** *(continued)*

ENVIRONMENTAL IMPACTS			
Impacts on	Key questions	Scenario I	Scenario II
		Impact assessment	
Climate	Does the instrument affect our ability to adapt to climate change?	As less untreated discharges are expected, some minor positive contribution to adaptation to possible climate change effects is expected.	It is unlikely that the small-scale pilot projects will significantly contribute to adapting to climate change.
Water quality and resources	Does the instrument decrease or increase the quality or quantity of freshwater and groundwater?	Quality of surface and groundwater is expected to marginally benefit from the scheme, either through better practice from the tourism sector and/or some additional investments in local water management – thanks to additional revenue.	No direct impact is expected. Financing improved protection of water bodies, particularly through respecting sanitary protection zones regimes of groundwater and spring water sources, will contribute to better quality of surface and groundwater.
	Does it affect drinking water resources?	Not directly.	No direct impact is expected. Financing improved protection of water bodies, particularly through respecting sanitary protection zones regimes of drinking water sources, will contribute to the protection of drinking water quality.
Land use	Does the instrument lead to a change in land use?	The instrument is not a game changer in terms of land use as it is marginal in effect.	Direct impact on land use is unlikely. Some impact on crop cultivation practices might occur as a result of implementation of good agricultural practices projects. The tourism sector, as well as protected areas systems, will greatly benefit from the implementation of pilot projects to improve water quantity and quality, and environmental quality.

Table C.2. **Surface water abstraction and water-body use charges (including non-consumptive uses)**

ECONOMIC AND FISCAL IMPACTS				
Impacts on	Key questions	Scenario I	Scenario IIb	Scenario IIa
		Impact assessment		
Business	Will the instrument pose an additional burden on local SMEs?	Marginal economic impacts are expected at general industry level by the introduction of the abstraction charge, knowing that Industrial organisations that are supplied with piped water by Vodokanals typically pay in the range of KGS 5 to 10 per cubic metre.	Very limited negative economic impact can be expected for fisheries and some industrial sectors.	

Table C.2. **Surface water abstraction and water-body use charges (including non-consumptive uses)** *(continued)*

ECONOMIC AND FISCAL IMPACTS				
Impacts on	Key questions	Scenario I	Scenario IIb	Scenario IIa
		Impact assessment		
Innovation and research	Will higher revenue for the sector correspond to higher investments in innovation and research?	Generation of additional revenue that can be re-allocated to water management (75%), but also to water monitoring, research and innovation in water efficiency (25%). The higher the charge, the higher the potential to contribute to innovation (from Scenario I, to IIa and then IIb).		
	Does it promote greater productivity and resource efficiency?	No effects are expected at this level of reform.	Promotion of innovation and increase of overall water efficiency levels, although most changes are expected from the increase in energy prices and pollution control measures.	Promotion of innovation and increase in overall water efficiency levels. Water use in industry is highly variable. Water pricing is only expected to have moderate influence in water efficiency compared to other drivers such as energy prices and pollution control regulation. Innovation stimulated by these various factors push towards new productive processes that involved higher water use efficiency, among others (Egenhofer et al., 2012). However, total water quantity used could increase beyond the present levels as water is made available by the efficiency measures implemented, new uses can be favoured, increasing the size of irrigated land (Jevons' paradox).
Consumers and households	Does the instrument have budgetary consequences for individual users and households?	Some impact can be expected on households and, consequently, on potentially vulnerable social groups. As the principal potential source of change, the electricity tariff would increase by around 5% from KGS 0.7 to 0.74 per kWh (OECD, 2013). However, this change, coupled with a marginal raise in water bills, does not substantially affect the affordability of both services.	Households' electricity bills are expected to increase, on average, by up to 5% (OECD, 2013). Thus, there will be impact on household budgets, but this is considered manageable using the proposed complementary measure (targeted social support to vulnerable households).	Electricity bills could increase by as much as some 20% (OECD, 2013), meaning a non-negligible economic impact on household budget. However, this is considered manageable using the proposed complementary measure.
Public budget	Does the instrument have budgetary consequences for public authorities at different levels of government?	The public budget is to be favoured according to each level of ambition of the scenarios. Revenue generated under this scenario would cover a significant part of the projected WRM expenditure presently heavily subsidised from the public budget.		

Table C.2. **Surface water abstraction and water-body use charges (including non-consumptive uses)** *(continued)*

ECONOMIC AND FISCAL IMPACTS				
Impacts on	Key questions	Scenario I	Scenario IIb	Scenario IIa
		Impact assessment		
Water utilities and irrigation service providers	How does the instrument financially affect water service companies and organisations?	The introduction of the charge will have an effect on water utilities, currently exempt from contributing for abstraction charges. However, this is expected to be transferred onto water users.		
Specific sectors	Would the instrument have a significant impact on specific sectors?	An economic impact can be expected for hydropower; however, this incremental cost is expected to be passed onto electricity users.	An economic impact can be expected for hydropower; however, this incremental cost is expected to be passed onto electricity users.	Same as Scenarios I and IIb, with the key addition of agriculture through the integration of the irrigation networks as contributors to the charge.

SOCIAL IMPACTS				
Impacts on	Key questions	Scenario I	Scenario IIb	Scenario IIa
		Impact assessment		
Vulnerable groups	Is the instrument affordable on average?	No perceptible changes are expected at this level of charge.	Current affordability levels of water supply services are not expected to change significantly. Current water bills from utilities are quite low, representing on average about 1.2% of disposable income in 2009 (CIS Statistics Committee, 2011). More recent samples (for 2011 and 2012) point at ratios that range from 1.2 to 5-6% within the poorest household quintile of several provincial towns. So changes beyond 2 to 3 times the current rates are expected to have an impact for a fraction of the poorest household quintile. For the wealthier households, water bills only represent about 0.2 to 0.7% of their income (see Annex A – 6: *Recent sample of the water bill expenditure to income ratio in regional cities across Kyrgyzstan* [*in 2011 and 2012*]).	Affordability levels of water supply services are not expected to change significantly. Current water bills from utilities are quite low, representing on average about 1.2% of disposable income in 2009 (CIS Statistics Committee, 2011). More recent samples (for 2011 and 2012) point at ratios that range from 1.2 to 5-6% within the poorest household quintile of several provincial towns. So changes beyond 2 to 3 times the current rates are expected to have an impact for a fraction of the poorest household quintile. For the wealthier households, water bills only represent about 0.2 to 0.7% of their income (see Annex A – 6: *Recent sample of the water bill expenditure to income ratio in regional cities across Kyrgyzstan* [*in 2011 and 2012*]).
	Is the instrument affordable for low-income groups?		Affordability issue for low-income groups will be addressed through targeted social support measures.	However, increased irrigation rates can have both direct and indirect impacts on rural households as food producers and water consumers. That said, currently the share of the expenditure for water in the total production costs are understood to be very low (probably less than 1% – according to the representative of the National Federation of Water User Associations), providing an important margin for increase.

Table C.2. **Surface water abstraction and water-body use charges (including non-consumptive uses)** *(continued)*

SOCIAL IMPACTS				
Impacts on	Key questions	Scenario I	Scenario IIb	Scenario IIa
		Impact assessment		
Participation	Does the instrument make the public better aware about sustainable water use and ecosystem protection?	This instrument does not affect users directly and is unlikely to substantially raise awareness and direct participation to WRM.		
Public health and safety	Does the instrument increase or decrease the likelihood of health risks due to substances harmful to the natural environment?	The instrument may contribute to this objective, but only indirectly through strengthened budgets for WRM in general.		

ENVIRONMENTAL IMPACTS				
Impacts on	Key questions	Scenario I	Scenario IIb	Scenario IIa
		Impact assessment		
Climate	Does the instrument affect our ability to adapt to climate change?	No significant effects are expected.	Improved water management budget is expected to have an increasingly positive environmental impact.	Improved water management is expected to have a strong positive environmental impact.
Water quality and resources	Does the instrument decrease or increase the quality or quantity of freshwater and groundwater?	At this level of charge, only marginal reductions in water use are expected.		
	Does it affect drinking water resources?	No significant effects are expected.	Indirect positive effects are expected.	
Land use	Does the instrument lead to a change in land use?	The instrument is not a game changer in terms of land use as it is marginal in effect.		At user level, water use is expected to decrease. However, the application at permit level is likely to entail a re-allocation of water use. The total abstracted quantity could increase beyond the permits (as water is made available, new uses can be favoured, such as increasing irrigated land – the Jevons' paradox [Polimeni et al., 2008]).

Table C.3. **Environmental pollution fees**

ECONOMIC AND FISCAL IMPACTS				
Impacts on	**Key questions**	**Scenario I**	**Scenario IIb**	**Scenario IIa**
		Impact assessment		
Business	Will the instrument pose an additional burden on local SMEs?	Application of fees at permit level (following their current review) with improved calculation of fee: *(i)* reduction of average monitoring and reporting costs for businesses and administrative costs for public administration.		Higher fees will have an initial negative impact on SMEs, and more so on the SME that are not able to review and update their process.
Innovation and research	Will higher revenue for the sector correspond to higher investments in innovation and research?	No changes are expected at these levels.	No changes are expected at these levels.	Clear promotion of innovation and increase of overall water treatment levels before discharge.
	Does it promote greater productivity and resource efficiency?	No changes are expected at these levels.		Clear promotion of innovation and increase of overall water treatment levels before discharge.
Consumers and households	Does the instrument have budgetary consequences for individual users and households?	As increasing fees are passed by Vodokanals onto final users and other economic producers, there are financial consequences for consumers. That said, an increase of tariffs is not incompatible with affordability concerns, given that current levels of tariffs are quite low. Moreover, for more ambitious scenarios, increased costs will be less of an issue as industries adapt their processes, becoming more efficient in general and lowering their operational costs in the long run.		
Public budget	Does the instrument have budgetary consequences for public authorities at different levels of government?	Generation of additional revenue: an improved collection of 50% from existing sources and an estimated 100% expected equivalent from Vodokanals.	Generation of additional revenue: an assumed improved collection of 50% from existing sources and an estimated 100% expected equivalent from Vodokanals and potential smaller contribution from other polluters.	
Water utilities and irrigation service providers	How does the instrument financially affect water service companies and organisations?	Vodokanals were exempt from this instrument so their introduction has an impact on utilities. Given the nature of their activity, this cost is likely to be passed onto consumers in the long term and partially covered by the public budget in the short term.		
Specific sectors	Would the instrument have a significant impact on specific sectors?	More impact can be expected in Bishkek and the Issyk-Kul Oblasts as they represent 45% and 28% of all current environmental fee revenue. Marginal economic impact is expected at the general industry level by the minimum reform.		More impact can be expected in Bishkek and the Issyk-Kul Oblast as they represent 45% and 28% of all current environmental fee revenue, respectively.

Table C.3. **Environmental pollution fees** *(continued)*

SOCIAL IMPACTS				
Impacts on	Key questions	Scenario I	Scenario IIb	Scenario IIa
		Impact assessment		
Vulnerable groups	Is the instrument affordable on average?	No substantial impact	Affordability levels of water supply services are not expected to change significantly.	
	Is the instrument affordable for low-income groups?	Some impact can be expected on households and, consequently, on potentially vulnerable social groups.	Some impact can be expected on households and, consequently, on potentially vulnerable social groups through the transfer of costs from Vodokanals. Current water bills are the lowest from utilities representing on average about 1.2% of disposable income in 2009 (CIS Statistics Committee, 2011). More recent samples (for 2011 and 2012) point at ratios that range from 1.2% to 5-6% within the poorest household quintile of several provincial towns. So changes beyond 2 to 3 times the current rates are expected to have an impact for a fraction of the poorest household quintile. For the wealthier households, water bills only represent about 0.7% to 0.2% of their income (see Annex A – 6: *Recent sample of the water bill expenditure to income ratio in regional cities across Kyrgyzstan [in 2011 and 2012]*).	
Participation	Does the instrument make the public better aware of sustainable water use and ecosystem protection?	The instrument does not directly affect end users of the resource.		
Public health and safety	Does the instrument increase or decrease the likelihood of health risks due to substances harmful to the natural environment?		Less-polluting discharges and improved water management are expected to have positive impacts on public health and safety, reducing water-borne infections (WBI) that are a burden for poor households which translates into: • high treatment costs (on average, KGS 1 450 per household – by all households) • lost school days (10 days, lost by each children from poor households) • foregone working days.	

ENVIRONMENTAL IMPACTS				
Impacts on	Key questions	Scenario I	Scenario IIb	Scenario IIa
		Impact assessment		
Climate	Does the instrument affect our ability to adapt to climate change?	No direct impact is expected.		Improved water management is expected to have a very strong positive environmental impact. At the level of the polluters, untreated quantities of water are expected to decrease.
Water quality and resources	Does the instrument decrease or increase the quality or quantity of freshwater and groundwater? Does it affect drinking water resources?	At this level of fees, no significant changes in pollution levels are expected, nor in the environment in general.	The fee is expected to start creating incentives for reducing untreated discharges with potential lower pollution levels, clearly beneficial for health and environment.	
Land use	Does the instrument lead to a change in land use?	No significant impact is expected.		

Table C.4. **Water supply and sanitation tariffs (case study)**

ECONOMIC AND FISCAL IMPACTS			
		Scenario I	**Scenario II**
Impacts on	**Key questions**	**Impact assessment**	
Business	Will the tariff increase pose an additional burden on local SMEs?	Not expected at this stage.	Larger users such as recreational/accommodation SMEs will face larger water bills, which are likely to be passed onto tourists.
Innovation and research	Will higher revenue for the sector correspond to higher investments in innovation and research?	Not expected from this instrument.	
	Does it promote greater productivity and resource efficiency?	Not expected at this stage.	Increase in the promotion of innovation towards more efficient water use. A more efficient use of water can be associated with lower energy use, given the importance of pumping costs. Higher tariffs are expected to raise individual efficiency, but a steadier availability of water associated with better infrastructure may increase total use of water.
Consumers and households	Does the instrument have budgetary consequences for individual users and households?	Given *(i)* the currently low water service expenditure to income ratio and *(ii)* the known willingness to pay for improved water supply, only marginal effects are expected in terms of affordability (see social impacts).	This longer-term scenario has budgetary consequences (see social impacts for affordability impacts).
Public budget	Does the instrument have budgetary consequences for public authorities at different levels of government?	Less dependence from operational subsidies offer more space for strengthening social programmes, if needed, as the reform will free some 5% of city budget. Tariff changes require local debate at the municipality council level (Kenesh) and may entail local transaction costs (but are expected to be lower than the benefits from the tariff increase).	Less dependence from operational subsidies offer more space for strengthening social programmes, if needed, as the reform will free some 5% of city budget. Tariff changes require local debate at the municipality-council level (Kenesh) and may entail some important transaction costs (but far lower than the benefits from the tariff increase).
Water utilities and irrigation service providers	How does the instrument financially affect water service companies and organisations?	Generation of additional revenue for the water utility. In the long run, it is expected to partially cover O&M costs.	Significant and strategic generation of additional revenue for the water utility.
Specific sectors	Would the tax increase have a significant impact on specific sectors?	All drinking water users will be affected by the changes.	

Table C.4. **Water supply and sanitation tariffs (case study)** *(continued)*

SOCIAL IMPACTS			
Impacts on	Key questions	Scenario I	Scenario II
		Impact assessment	
Vulnerable groups	Is the tariff increase affordable on average? Is the tariff increase affordable for low-income groups?	Only if the income/water bill ratio is close to 2.5% can this change become a burden on the poorest households, but it is unlikely at this level of tariff.	Affordability levels of water supply services are expected to change significantly, at least in nominal terms. Two aspects need to be highlighted: the increase in the water supply tariff and the expansion of the sewerage services, meaning that an increasing share of the population will be paying for a new service. It is the new service that is expected to have a negative impact on the poorest of households. Current water bills are the lowest from all utilities representing on average about 1.2% of disposable income in 2009 (CIS Statistics Committee, 2011). More recent samples (for 2011 and 2012) point at ratios that range from 5-6% to 1.2% within the poorest household quintile of several provincial towns. So changes beyond 2 to 3 times the current rates are expected to have an impact for a fraction of the poorest household quintile. For the wealthier households, water bills only represent about 0.7-0.2% of their income (see Annex A – 6: *Recent sample of the water bill expenditure to income ratio in regional cities across Kyrgyzstan* [*in 2011 and 2012*]*)*. However, improved WSS services can bring two benefits associated with health benefits. In the short/medium term, as the incidence of water-borne infections goes down, households would experience lower medical bills (immediate financial benefits). In the longer term, larger economic benefits are associated with a healthier population able to work more productively (but assessing these long-term benefits is beyond the scope of this report).
Participation	Does the instrument make the public better aware of sustainable water use and ecosystem protection?	The evolution and reform of tariffs are an opportunity to communicate on the issue and challenges of water management. Any reform of this kind should also be accompanied by a communication strategy and campaign (refer to Action Plan).	
Public health and safety	Does the instrument increase or decrease the likelihood of health risks due to substances harmful to the natural environment?	n.a.	Water-borne infections (WBI) are controlled, generating value for all and particularly for the poorest segments of the population.

Table C.4. **Water supply and sanitation tariffs (case study)** *(continued)*

ENVIRONMENTAL IMPACTS			
Impacts on	Key questions	Scenario I	Scenario II
		Impact assessment	
Climate	Does the instrument affect our ability to adapt to climate change?	Unlikely at this stage.	A more efficient use of water can be associated with lower energy use, given the importance of pumping costs.
Water quality and resources	Does the instrument decrease or increase the quality or quantity of freshwater and groundwater?	At this level of fees, no significant changes in water-level usage are expected.	Higher tariffs are expected to raise individual efficiency, but a steadier availability of water associated with better infrastructure may increase total use of water.
	Does it affect drinking water resources?	Water availability is more stable across the system thanks to investments, which are indirectly related to higher tariffs.	
Land use	Does the instrument lead to a change in land use?	There is no direct impact on land use expected from changes on tariff themselves. However, investments and improvement of the network in previously neglected or not-served areas may attract more urban development with its associated environmental pressures around the lake.	

Table C.5. **Irrigation fees**

ECONOMIC AND FISCAL IMPACTS						
Impacts on	Key questions	Scenario 0	Scenario Ia	Scenario Ib	Scenario IIb	Scenario IIa
		Impact assessment				
Business	Will the instrument pose an additional burden on local SMEs?	The instrument will only fully implement the existing regulation. The current payment rate of SME is unknown.	The very gradual increase is expected to have only negligible effects in real terms.	Increasing fees has implication for SMEs, but as this water is an intermediate good, fees are expected to be transferred onto consumers of agricultural products, including food products.		
Innovation and research	Will higher revenue for the sector correspond to higher investments in innovation and research?	Not expected.	Not expected.	Marginal contribution.		Potential contribution to investment in innovation.
	Does it promote greater productivity and resource efficiency?			Marginal contribution.	There is an incentive for innovation towards more efficient use of water.	Increase in the promotion of innovation towards more water efficiency use. Energy use is to be made more efficient.
Consumers and households	Does the instrument have budgetary consequences for individual users and households?	Not expected.	Indirect effect on household use for domestic purposes of irrigation water can be expected, but these are negligible both given the level changes and the importance of this source for direct household consumption.			

Table C.5. **Irrigation fees** *(continued)*

ECONOMIC AND FISCAL IMPACTS						
Impacts on	Key questions	Scenario 0	Scenario Ia	Scenario Ib	Scenario IIb	Scenario IIa
		Impact assessment				
Public budget	Does the instrument have budgetary consequences for public authorities at different levels of government?	Yes. Revenue is expected to double compared to the current levels. But even more funding is required. Public funds can be reallocated, for example to support further reform of the fees.	On the basis on the improvements from Scenario 0, changes in the fee rates can be implemented at low transaction costs for public administration.	Additional revenue will gradually strengthen the overall budget for irrigation services. Additional efforts for the establishment of the two-part tariff system are expected, raising transaction costs.	Additional revenue will gradually strengthen the overall budget for irrigation services.	Additional revenue will gradually strengthen the overall budget for irrigation services.
Water utilities and irrigation service providers	How does the instrument financially affect water service companies and organisations?	The main effect is less reliance on public funds for this particular service. Existing public support can be allocated to support reform.	Generation of additional revenue over time to partially cover O&M costs.	Following scenarios 0 and Ia, this scenario should be a key milestone of reform in the medium term with the introduction of a two-part tariff system. In terms of service, more stable income is expected to translate in more stable water availability across the system.	Revenue levels ensure coverage of the O&M costs.	Revenue levels ensure high levels of O&M costs coverage.
Specific sectors	Would the instrument have a significant impact on specific sectors?	All changes and implications will naturally affect agriculture.				

SOCIAL IMPACTS						
Impacts on	Key questions	Scenario 0	Scenario Ia	Scenario Ib	Scenario IIb	Scneario IIa
		Impact assessment				
Vulnerable groups	Is the instrument affordable on average?	Current fee levels are understood to be very low.	Given the known willingness to pay for irrigation water, only marginal effects are expected in terms of affordability.	Affordability levels of irrigation water supply services are not expected to change significantly, however less dependence from operational subsidies offer more space to social programmes if needed.	However, increased irrigation rates can have both direct and indirect impacts on rural households as food producers and water consumers. That said, the current share of expenditure for water in the total production costs of water is understood to be very low (probably less than 1% – according to a representative of the National Federation of Water Users' Associations), providing an important margin for increase.	
	Is the instrument affordable for low-income groups?					
Participation	Does the instrument make the public better aware of sustainable water use and ecosystem protection?	An increase in the collection rate is expected to raise the profile of WRM and its budget requirements.	Same as Scenario 0, but with a more acute message to users through increasingly higher fees.			

Table C.5. **Irrigation fees** *(continued)*

SOCIAL IMPACTS						
Impacts on	Key questions	Scenario 0	Scenario Ia	Scenario Ib	Scenario IIb	Scneario IIa
		Impact assessment				
Public health and safety	Does the instrument increase or decrease the likelihood of health risks due to substances harmful to the natural environment?	No major direct implication for this dimension.				

ENVIRONMENTAL IMPACTS						
Impacts on	Key questions	Scenario 0	Scenario Ia	Scenario Ib	Scenario IIb	Scenario IIa
		Impact assessment				
Climate	Does the instrument affect our ability to adapt to climate change?	No significant contribution.	Improved and more autonomous budget contributes to increase resilience from the system.		Water supply is more dependable across the system and is less vulnerable to climate change.	
Water quality and resources	Does the instrument decrease or increase the quality or quantity of freshwater and groundwater?	Not expected.	At this level of fees, no significant changes in water level usage are expected.	Water availability is more stable across the system.		
	Does it affect drinking water resources?		Not expected.	As some irrigation water can be used for drinking purposes, these scenarios may improve access to the resource.		
Land use	Does the instrument lead to a change in land use?		Not expected.		At the level of the single user, water use is expected to decrease. However, total quantity used could increase beyond the present levels as water is made available by the efficiency measures implemented, new uses can be favoured, such as increasing irrigated land (Jevons' paradox).	

Table C.6. **Product tax/recycling fee/import duty on pesticides**

ECONOMIC AND FISCAL IMPACTS			
Impacts on	Key questions	Scenario I	Scenario II
		Impact assessment	
Bus ness	Will the tax (import duty) increase pose an additional burden for local SMEs?	Input increased costs are expected to affect farming SMEs, however, this increase is expected to be absorbed through practice adaptations of pest control strategies, as long as the suggested tax rates are high enough.	
Innovation and research	Will higher revenue for the sector correspond to higher investments in innovation and research?	Part of the revenue from the tax may be invested in innovation to move from a pesticide-intense pest control strategy to alternative practices.	
	Does it promote greater productivity and resource efficiency?	The instrument is expected to shift use from highly toxic to less toxic products.	This scenario is looking to reduce the use of pesticides per hectare.

Table C.6. **Product tax/recycling fee/import duty on pesticides** *(continued)*

ECONOMIC AND FISCAL IMPACTS			
Impacts on	Key questions	Scenario I	Scenario II
		Impact assessment	
Consumers and households	Does the instrument have budgetary consequences for individual users and households?	Most changes are expected to be absorbed by producers in the medium term through the adaptation of the pest control strategy of farmers.	
Public budget	Does the instrument have budgetary consequences for public authorities at different levels of government?	As (entirely imported) pesticides do not currently generate any fiscal revenue, the introduction of a tax (import duty) will positively contribute to the budget, and increasingly so as the implementation goes from Scenario I to II. However, the fiscal income is expected to stabilise (or even decrease) over a very long term, as the pesticide use per hectare will likely decrease.	
Water utilities and irrigation service providers	How does the instrument financially affect water service companies and organisations?	No direct effects are expected from this instrument.	
Specific sectors	Would the tax increase have a significant impact on specific sectors?	Agriculture is the main sector to be affected by this reform. Input price increase is expected to have an effect on farmers' income. However, this effect is expected to be absorbed in the long term through adaptations of pest control strategies, as long as the suggested tax rates are high enough and farmers are in a position to successfully revise their practices.	

SOCIAL IMPACTS			
Impacts on	Key questions	Scenario I	Scenario II
		Impact assessment	
Vulnerable groups	Is the instrument introduction affordable on average? Is the instrument introduction affordable for low-income groups?	Subsistence farmers are the most vulnerable group likely to be directly affected. However, they are less likely to be capital intensive in terms of inputs, and proportionally less dependent on pesticides. This dimension requires a detailed analysis of: • the level of dependence on pesticides of small-scale subsistence farmers (48% of the population of Kyrgyzstan is employed by the agriculture sector) • the general price elasticity (changes in the use of pesticides by farmers in response to changes in the prices of pesticides).	
Participation	Does the instrument make the public better aware of sustainable water use and ecosystem protection?	The public is not directly affected by the instrument, therefore does not a direct effect on participation or awareness.	
Public health and safety	Does the instrument increase or decrease the likelihood of health risks due to substances harmful to the natural environment?	Both scenarios reduce health risks associated with pesticide use and pollution.	

Table C.6. **Product tax/recycling fee/import duty on pesticides** *(continued)*

ENVIRONMENTAL IMPACTS			
		Scenario I	Scenario II
Impacts on	Key questions	Impact assessment	
Climate	Does the instrument affect our ability to adapt to climate change?	Lower dependence on energy-intensive inputs are an advantage and do support adaptation to climate change. In addition, and possibly more importantly, the development of alternative pest control strategies may offer more flexible alternatives than conventional spreading to evolving phyto-sanitary threats brought about climate change.	
Water quality and resources	Does the instrument decrease or increase the quality or quantity of freshwater and groundwater?	Lower quantities of diffuse pollutants are expected to have positive effects on the quality of drinking water sources. However, direct effects are to be monitored locally.	
	Does it affect drinking water resources?	No changes in quantities of water are expected. However, if the sensitivity of farmers to higher input prices (i.e. pesticides) entails changes to more or less water-intensive crops, then the instrument could have marginal water quantity effects as well.	
Land use	Does the instrument lead to a change in land use?	Type of crops could be changed in the adaptation of pest control strategies, even promoting changes from/to annual crops from/ to perennial ones.	The land-change uses effect may be lower under Scenario II than in Scenario I.

Table C.7. **Import duty on lubricants (to tackle the issue of waste oils)**

ECONOMIC AND FISCAL IMPACTS			
		Scenario I	Scenario II
Impacts on	Key questions	Impact assessment	
Business	Will the import duty increase pose an additional burden for local SMEs?	The additional cost (about KGS 3.75/kg) of product is to be shared among all users.	
Innovation and research	Will higher revenue for the sector correspond to higher investments in innovation and research?	Part of the revenue from the tax may be invested in innovation to establish the basis of a functioning (and formal) market for waste oil.	In the case of Scenario II, resources are to potentially have a more direct influence on innovation as they could be invested in the uptake of waste oil regeneration technologies to produce new oils and purified fuels locally.
	Does it promote greater productivity and resource efficiency?	Under this scenario, the instrument is not to have a direct impact on resource efficiency.	At this stage, the structure of the import duty is expected to favour more easily-manageable waste products and therefore directly contribute to resource efficiency throughout the life cycle of the product.
Consumers and households	Does the instrument have budgetary consequences for individual users and households?	Most changes are expected to be absorbed by users in the medium term.	
Public budget	Does the instrument have budgetary consequences for public authorities at different levels of government?	As lubricants are entirely imported, the introduction of a specific import duty will positively contribute to the budget. However, the fiscal income is not expected to contribute to other objectives than to manage waste oils. In time, and although the number of vehicles is expected to increase, the quantities individually used may decrease in time due to technological improvement in the quality of the lubricants and the performance of modern engine technology.	
Water utilities and irrigation service providers	How does the instrument financially affect water service companies and organisations?	No direct effects are expected from this instrument.	
Specific sectors	Would the tax increase have a significant impact on specific sectors?	The system is not expected to impact a particular sector. However, the use of the resources gathered could contribute to the formal establishment of a new sector in the waste management industry.	

Table C.7. **Import duty on lubricants (to tackle the issue of waste oils)** *(continued)*

SOCIAL IMPACTS			
Impacts on	Key questions	Scenario I	Scenario II
		Impact assessment	
Vulnerable groups	Is the instrument introduction affordable on average?	Although all users of motorised vehicles are expected to bear the burden of the import duty, no significant change in the cost of using motorised vehicles is to be expected.	
	Is the instrument introduction affordable for low-income groups?		
Participation	Does the instrument make the public better aware of sustainable water use and ecosystem protection?	The public is not directly affected by the instrument, therefore it has no direct effect on participation or awareness.	
Public health and safety	Does the instrument increase or decrease the likelihood of health risks due to substances harmful to the natural environment?	Both scenarios reduce health risks associated with waste oil pollution.	

ENVIRONMENTAL IMPACTS			
Impacts on	Key questions	Scenario I	Scenario II
		Impact assessment	
Climate	Does the instrument affect our ability to adapt to climate change?	In time, a more efficient life cycle of lubricants and oils represents, although modestly, a contribution to climate change mitigation, but not so much for adaptation.	
Water quality and resources	Does the instrument decrease or increase the quality or quantity of freshwater and groundwater?	Lower quantities of diffuse pollutants are expected to have positive effects on the quality of drinking water sources. However, direct effects are to be monitored locally. No changes in quantities of water are expected.	
	Does it affect drinking water resources?		
Land use	Does the instrument lead to a change in land use?	No effects of this type are expected.	

Annex D

Reference data

Table D.1. **Cost estimate of water supply services of Cholpon-Ata Vodokanal (excluding VAT and sales tax)**

No.	Items	Unit	Costs		Including for			
					Groundwater		Surface water	
			Overall	Per 1 m³	Overall	Per 1 m³	Overall	Per 1 m³
1	Expenditure							
	Material expenses and services, including:							
	Raw stock and materials, chlorine and reagents	*000 KGS*	*221.3*	*0.31*	*110.7*	*0.25*	*110.7*	*0.43*
	Electricity power	*000 KGS*	*2 332.7*	*3.29*	*2 315.3*	*5.15*	*17.4*	*0.07*
	Fuel and lubricants	*000 KGS*	*174.8*	*0.25*	*87.4*	*0.19*	*87.4*	*0.34*
	Hiring machinery, transport, services outsourcing	*000 KGS*	*151.5*	*0.21*	*143.5*	*0.32*	*8.0*	*0.03*
	R&M of Fixed Assets*	*000 KGS*	*241.8*	*0.34*	*241.8*	*0.54*		
	Water Management Services (DWM&M)	*000 KGS*	*254.6*	*0.36*			*254.6*	*0.98*
	Sub-total 1:		3 376.7	4.76	2 898.7	6.45	478.1	1.85
	Salary cost	000 KGS	2 774.9	3.91	1 576.4	3.50	1198.5	4.62
	Social insurance tax	000 KGS	478.7	0.67	271.9	0.60	206.7	0.80
	Depreciation	000 KGS	163.2	0.23	152.6	0.34	10.6	0.04
	Royalty tax	000 KGS	216.7	0.31	216.7	0.48		
	VAT not subject to offset		92.6	0.13	46.3	0.10	46.3	0.18
	Other expenses	000 KGS	213.3	0.30			213.3	0.82
	Total direct cost	000 KGS	7 316.1	10.31	5 162.6	11.47	2 153.5	8.31
	Share in total cost	Percentage			70.6		29.4	
	General administrative and running costs	000 KGS	1 195.3	1.68	843.5	1.87	351.6	1.36
	Total costs	000 KGS	8 511.4	11.99	6 006.1	13.34	2 505.1	9.67
2	Quantity of water supply	000 m³	709.4		449.9		259.6	
	Cost of 1 m³ of water	KGS		12.00		13.40		9.65
3	Revenue	000 KGS	5 862.0		4 522.7		1 339.2	
	Share in total revenue	Percentage			77.2		22.8	
	Average tariff for 1 m³ including for population:	KGS		8.26		10.05		5.16
	Financial result (profit/loss)	000 KGS	-2 649.4		-1 483.3		-1 166.1	
	Production profitability	Percentage	-31.1		-24.7		-46.5	

***R&M**: repair and maintenance.

Source: Cholpon-Ata Vodokanal data.

Table D.2. **Cost estimate of sanitation services of Cholpon-Ata Vodokanal (excluding VAT and sales tax)**

No.	Items	Unit	Costs: Overall	Costs: Per 1m³
1	Expenditure			
	Material expenses and services, including:			
	Raw stock and materials, chlorine and reagents	*000 KGS*	*157.4*	*0.56*
	Electricity power	*000 KGS*	*407.4*	*1.46*
	Fuel and lubricants	*000 KGS*	*101.1*	*0.36*
	R&M of fixed assets*	*000 KGS*		
	Hiring machinery, transport, services outsourcing	*000 KGS*	*16.5*	*0.06*
	Other expenses	*000 KGS*	*109.9*	*0.39*
	Sub-total 1:		792.3	2.83
	Salary cost	000 KGS	1 762.7	6.30
	Social insurance tax	000 KGS	304.1	1.09
	Depreciation	000 KGS	489.6	1.75
	VAT not subject to offset			
	Total direct cost	000 KGS	3 348.7	11.97
	General administrative and running costs	000 KGS	549.4	1.96
	Total costs	000 KGS	3 898.1	13.93
2	Quantity of effluents	000 m³	279.7	
	Cost of 1 m³ of effluents	KGS		13.94
3	Revenue	000 KGS	4 633.9	
	Average tariff for 1 m³ including for population:	KGS		16.57
	Financial result (profit/loss)	000 KGS	735.8	
	Production profitability	Percentage	18.9	

***R&M**: repair and maintenance.
Source: Cholpon-Ata Vodokanal data.

Table D.3. **Number of connections to water supply network of Cholpon-Ata Municipal Enterprise Vodokanal (as of 1 September 2012)**

Customers of Cholpon-Ata Municipal Enterprise "Vodokanal"	No.	Meters	Meters needed	Estimated population	Unit consumption, lcd	Estimated consumption m³/day
Population – 4 092 connections	4 092	90		16 368	150	2 455.20
Small hotels – 189 connections (including 40 with water meters installed)	189	40	149	2 362.5	300	708.75
Organisations – 61 (including 28 with water meters installed)	61	28	33		2 000	122.00
Grocery shops – 21 (including 2 with water meters installed)	21	2	19		250	5.25
Cafes – 14 (including 12 with water meters installed)	14	12	2		1 000	14.00
Beauty salons – 6 (including 4 with water meters installed)	6	4	2		500	3.00
Bakeries – 6 (including 5 with water meters installed)	6	5	1		500	3.00
Car washing shops – 5 (including 2 with water meters installed)	5	2	3		2 000	10.00
Others (seasonal) – 25 (including 3 with water meters installed)	25	3	22		1 000	25.00
Total number of connections:	**4 419**	**186**	**231**	**18 731**		**3 346**

Note: **lcd**: litres per capita per day.

Source: Cholpon-Ata Vodokanal data.

Table D.4. **Household income and cash expenditure per capita in the Issyk-Kul Oblast (KGS per month) in 2012**

Income
(average per capita, in KGS per month)

	Issyk-Kul Oblast		
	Total	**Urban**	**Rural**
Revenue – total	**3 130.0**	**3 375.2**	**3 035.4**
Salary	1 316.1	1 791.2	1 132.8
Individual business activities	301.0	574.1	195.6
Odd jobs	17.1	4.6	21.9
Revenue outside the territory of Kyrgyzstan	112.7	67.7	130.1
Income from property	35.3	104.3	8.7
Scholarships	0.3	1.1	0.0
Pensions	573.9	575.7	573.2
Social aid	14.3	16.8	13.3
Income from our land spot	682.2	149.0	887.9
Other income	77.1	90.7	71.8
Reference:			
Proceeds from bank accounts	0.0	0.0	0.0
Credits, loans	38.7	7.1	50.9

Cash expenditure
(average per capita, in KGS per month)

	Issyk-Kul Oblast		
	Total	**Urban**	**Rural**
Total consumption	**2 645.01**	**3 095.92**	**2 471.04**
For consumption	**2 263.70**	**2 698.02**	**2 096.14**
Commodity	1 357.44	1 566.69	1 276.71
Nourishment out of home	9.03	22.06	4.01
Alcohol	11.55	7.21	13.22
Tobacco	20.06	13.68	22.52
Clothing, footwear, linen and fabric	276.40	297.42	268.29
Personal hygiene items	74.41	84.31	70.60
Furniture	8.87	10.41	8.28
Purchase of vehicles	4.72	5.33	4.49
Fuel	80.41	142.99	56.26
Housing and communal services	82.13	119.98	67.52
Health	40.43	53.19	35.50
Pre-school education	5.17	14.43	1.60
Education services	34.08	35.16	33.67
Services of culture institutions	0.25	0.84	0.03
Public transport services	44.33	54.98	40.22
Communication services	66.04	83.56	59.28
Miscellaneous goods and services	148.39	185.78	133.96
Other expenses	**381.31**	**397.89**	**374.90**
Expenditure on private farming	86.81	32.14	107.91
Financial assistance to relatives and another	99.05	89.60	102.70
Deposits in banking institutions	0.00	0.00	0.00
Purchase of foreign currency	0.20	0.73	0.00
Construction and real estate purchase	0.00	0.00	0.00
Taxes, fees and other payments	192.05	263.97	164.30
Other expenses	3.19	11.46	0.00

Source: National Statistics Committee, a sample survey of households (for the year 2012).

Recent sample of the water bill expenditure to income ratio in regional cities across Kyrgyzstan (in 2011 and 2012)

Karabalta City, Chui Oblast

At the beginning of 2011, Karabalta had an estimated 38 557 inhabitants, living in around 13 550 households. The official population figures suggest that an average household size in Karabalta City is 2.8 persons. This is **abnormally low** for the Kyrgyz Republic and for the remainder of Chui Oblast and may reflect that people of working age have left the town to seek employment elsewhere, leaving only the young and the elderly. By the end of 2010, the Karabalta City Administration had registered 4.2% of households as extremely poor households, having an income of KGS 986.60 or less per capita per month; approximately 20% were named as poor households, having an income of KGS 986.61-1 618.00 per capita per month. Many not already connected are very likely to find it difficult to pay for the full amount at one time for a connection to the piped water supply, and possibly to the sewerage system. However, if allowed, they may be able to pay in installments.

Households included in the small household survey indicated their annual expenditure for water and wastewater constituted from 2.7% of the total annual expenditure for the lowest quintile (i.e. the 20% of households with the lowest annual income) to 1.3% of the total expenditure for the highest quintile households (i.e. the 20% of households with the annual highest income). Therefore, most households could afford to pay a higher monthly bill for the water (and wastewater) bill. Many participants in the household survey and the focus group discussions also indicated they are willing to pay more for improved water supply services.

Talas City, Talas Oblast

Table D.5. **Tariff for water and sewerage, in KGS**

	Water, 1 m^3	Sewerage, 1 m^3
Households	3.20	-
Budgetary organisations	13.30	7.40
Commercial and industrial users	21.80	9.50

Source: Vodokanal data.

Information from household survey and focus group discussions (May-June 2012)

Most household survey data were analysed by expenditure quintile, with quintile 1 being the 20% of households with the lowest level of annual expenditure and quintile 5 being the 20% of households with the highest level of expenditure. **The average monthly expenditure for domestic water constituted 0.4% of the total expenditure of all survey households, with households in quintile 1 using a slightly higher proportion of their expenditure for domestic water (0.6%) than other households.** The survey households who had either an in-house or a yard connection to the centralised (piped) water supply reported using a higher proportion of their income on water supply than other households, but still only averaging 0.7% of their monthly expenditure. Households in quintile 1 with an in-house or a yard connection used 1.3% of their monthly expenditure to pay their water bills.

The average expenditure for all survey households for wastewater services, including emptying septic tanks, constituted 0.1% of their total expenditure. The survey households with a connection to the centralised wastewater system used on average the same proportion of their expenditure on wastewater services as other households.

Moreover, 42% of the survey households not connected to the centralised water supply said they would be able and willing to pay for a connection (costing KGS 10 000 or more), if they would be provided with enough and good-quality water. Most of them (84%) would be able to pay the whole amount at the same time. Many of the poor not already connected are likely to find it difficult to pay the full amount at one time for a connection to the centralised water supply, and/or possibly to the centralised wastewater system, but may be able to pay if allowed to pay in instalments. However, most likely some very poor households will not be able to afford a connection, even when paying in installments. For these households, access to a street tap located within a reasonable distance from the dwelling may remain the best solution.

Osh City, Osh Oblast

Results from the household survey indicate a negative correlation between family size and income level: the larger the family, the lower their (per capita) income. Households with many children tend to be poorer.

Table D.6. **Average income related to family size**

Average HH income in KGS	Average number of HH members	Average income/HH member in KGS
8 389	5.67	1 479
10 210	4.55	2 244
12 124	4.22	2 873
13 137	3.64	3 609
14 908	2.64	5 647

Source: Project Household Survey (2012).

Average per capita income amounts to KGS 3 300/month, average expenditure KGS 2 400 /month. Average per capita income of urban dwellers (in the 10 settlements) is on average 1.5 times larger than income of rural dwellers (Japalak). Some 6% of urban households receive financial support from relatives. A significant share of income comes from remittances by migrant workers. The largest share of household income in Japalak comes from agricultural activities.

Expenditure for public utilities (gas, electricity, water, sewerage) represents on 8% for urban households and about 2% in Japalak where there are no gas connections and availability of water connections is limited. Average monthly per capita expenditure for water and sewerage is KGS 35– that is about 1.5% of average total expenses or about 1% of total household income.

Table D.7. **Percentage of monthly income per person spent on water and sewerage services**

	Monthly per capita income in KGS		Number of HHs in the sample	Number of persons in the HHs	Percentage monthly per capita expenditure for water and sewerage services based on average KGS 35/person/month		Payment for *Vodokanal* tariff in KGS September 2010
Quintiles	Minimum	Maximum			Maximum	Minimum	
Quintile 1	600	2 803	60	316	5.83	1.25	79
Quintile 2	2 100	2 833	61	274	1.67	1.24	
Quintile 3	2 875	3 500	59	239	1.22	1.00	
Quintile 4	3 533	4 500	60	206	0.99	0.78	74
Quintile 5	4 600	15 000	60	144	0.76	0.23	
Total			300	1 179			

Source: Household survey and own calculations.

The difference in percentages may be smaller since wealthier families are more likely to live in apartments in multi-story buildings where the current tariff is KGS 11.64-39.18 per person per month; families living in private houses do not pay for sewerage (for them, the payment for drinking water varies between KGS 3.43 and KGS 6.15 per person per month depending on whether the tap is in the street or in the yard). On the other hand, families in private houses are more likely to pay for water supply for irrigation and their livestock. Household survey data show that households in private houses pay almost twice as much as residents in apartments, although the tariffs are usually lower.

Jalal-Abat City, Jalal-Abat Oblast

Jalalabad, the capital city of the Jalalabad Oblast is the country's third-largest urban settlement. It had some 98 500 inhabitants in 2010, including the rural council Taigaraev, in 21 900 households. The city covers an area of about 45 km^2. The Jalalabad self-government includes the municipality/municipal council, five territorial councils and quarter committees (villages in the rural Taigaraev).

The average size of a family is estimated at 4.5. About one-third of the families includes five persons or more; the larger the family, the lower the per capita income. Education levels are relatively high with reportedly 93% having completed secondary education and higher. Monthly per capita income varies between KGS 575 and 20 000 and averages KGS 3 400/month. Average per capita expenditure is KGS 2 700/month.

Expenditure for public utilities (gas, electricity, water, sewerage) averages 7% from total expenditure for urban territorial councils and 4% for Taigaraev. Per capita expenditure for water and sewerage services amounts to about KGS 35/month and takes about 1.3% from the average monthly expenses and about 1% from average monthly income (maximum 6% for the poor and 0.2% for the wealthy households).

About half of households comprise 1-3 persons. However, about one-third are relatively large, comprising five persons or more. Survey results indicate a negative correlation between family size and income levels; the larger the family, the lower their (per capita) income; the households have been divided into five quintiles based on their per capita incomes. Households with many children tend to be poorer.

Table D.8. **Average Incomes related to the size of surveyed households**

Average number of HH members	Average HH income, in KGS	Average income per HH member, in KGS
5.58	11 132	1 995
5.25	11 975	2 281
4.26	11 502	2 700
3.66	13 220	3 612
2.32	12 683	5 467

Source: Household Survey.

Average per capita income amounts to KGS 3 400/month, average expenditure to KGS 2 700/month. The average figure can be misleading. In fact, only 1.4% households reported they can actually save and had some savings. Average per capita income of urban dwellers is 1.6 times higher than of rural dwellers (in Taigaraev). A significant share of income comes from remittances (between 16-20%). The relatively largest share of household income in Taigaraev is from agricultural activities. While one-third of income of relatively wealthy households is from private entrepreneurship, the largest share of income of relatively poor households is from salaries. Expenses for mobile communication exceed expenses for health and education in all income groups.

Expenditure for public utilities (gas, electricity, water, sewerage) averages 7% for the four urban settlement and 4% in Taigaraev where there are no heating, gas or sewerage connections; public water supply connections are few. Average monthly per capita expenditure for water and sewerage is KGS 35/month, i.e. about 1.3% of average total expenses or about 1% of average monthly income.

Table D.9. **Monthly per capita expenditure for water and sewerage services in percentage of monthly per capita income**

	Monthly per capita income, in KGS				Monthly per capita expenditure for water and sewerage services based on average KGS 35 per person per month, in percentage of monthly per capita income	
Quintiles	Minimum	Maximum	Number of HHs in the sample	Number of persons in the HHs	Maximum	Minimum
Quintile 1	575	2 233	60	344	6.0	1.6
Quintile 2	2 250	2 857	60	287	1.6	1.2
Quintile 3	2 867	3 750	60	212	1.2	0.9
Quintile 4	3 833	5 000	63	191	0.9	0.7
Quintile 5	5 333	20 000	57	113	0.6	0.2
Total			300	1 147		

Source: Household survey and own calculations.

These estimates are based on averages; the difference in percentages may in some cases be smaller since wealthier families are more likely to live in MSB apartments with connection to sewerage where the current tariff is KGS 40.62/person/month; families in MSBs without sewerage connection or in private houses should pay between KGS 4.89-23.74/month/person. On the other hand, households living in family houses are likely to be larger and to pay more for water supply for irrigation and their livestock. The data suggest that households from the survey sample residing in private houses can pay almost twice as much as residents in MSBs. It also shows that none of the categories pays full tariff.

Table D.10. **Selected water and sewage tariffs (in KGS)**

	2009			2010		
Service	Households	Industry and commerce	Budgetary entities	Households	Industry and commerce	Budgetary entities
Water	5.40	7.30	5.40	7.30	5.40	7.30
Sewerage	3.60	4.90	3.60	4.90	3.60	4.90

Source: Vodokanal data.

Since there is no metering either at production or consumer levels, water and sewage bills are calculated based on per capita consumption norms inherited from Soviet times. They also depend on other use of water.

Number of vehicles in Kyrgyzstan

According to the General Directorate of Traffic Safety at the Ministry of Internal Affairs of the Kyrgyz Republic, the number of transportation means (trucks, cars, motorbikes, etc.) as per beginning of 2014 is more than 900 000 units.

The graph in Figure D.1 shows the evolution of the number of vehicles for 2005-10.

Figure D.1. **Evolution of the number of vehicles in Kyrgyzstan**

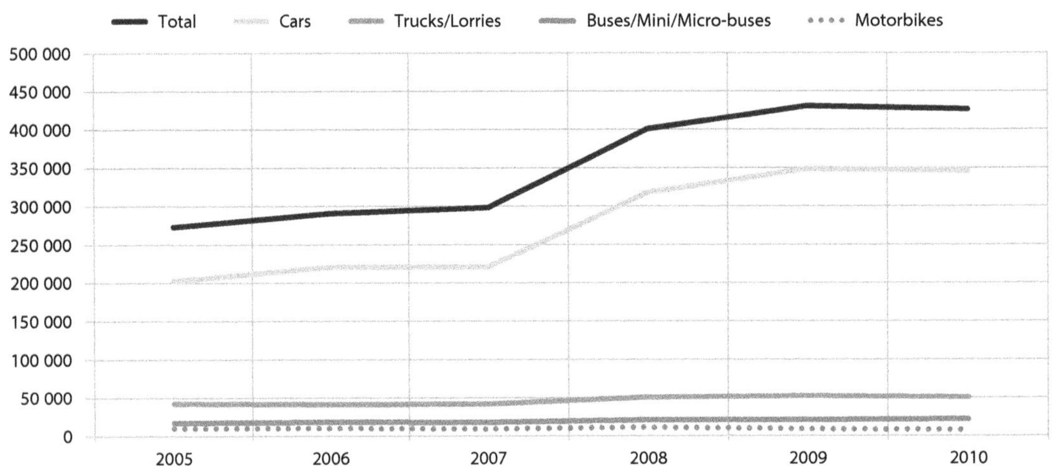

Source: General Directorate of Traffic Safety at Ministry of Internal Affairs of the Kyrgyz Republic, National Statistics Committee.

Table D.11. **Basic statistics on engine lubricants for a sample of European countries**

Country	Quantities of oil/ lubricants purchased	Used tonnes	Collected tonnes	Population as of 2013	Kg/capita	Vehicles	Kg/vehicle
Finland	70 074	45 000	34 200	5 426 674	82 923 721	332 1124	13 54 962 759
Denmark	61 182	28 000	20 000	5 602 628	49 976 547	2 689 261	10 41 178 057
Bulgaria	156 000	73 800	5 455	7 284 552	10 131 028	2 862 829	257 786 971
Portugal	93 576	41 169	31 695	10 487 289	39 256 094	5 747 034	7 163 520 754
Greece	81 100	39 000	23 790	11 062 508	35 254 212	6 903 005	5 649 713 428
Belgium	110 742	46 710	44 711	11 161 642	41 848 681	6 239 358	7 486 347 299
Netherlands	115 412	54 000	54 000	16 779 575	32 181 983	8 859 616	6 095 072 567
Poland	311 000	160 000	80 000	38 533 299	41 522 528	20 692 382	7 732 314 403
Estonia	485 200	190 000	180 000	46 704 308	40 681 472	27 695 655	6 860 281 963
Italy	529 870	227 371	212 497	59 685 227	38 095 021	40 526 269	5 610 459 706
United Kingdom	800 000	440 000	350 000	63 887 988	68 870 536	33 157 866	1 326 985 286
France	507 911	300 000	240 000	65 633 194	45 708 578	37 935 986	7 908 058 564
Germany	1 079 576	493 000	493 000	80 523 746	61 224 176	46 059 583	10 70 352 728

Source: Used tones of lubricants and collected volumes (BIOIS, 2010), Population of sample countries (Eurostat), adapted number of vehicles (World Bank data), estimates per capita and vehicles by authors.

Table D.12. **Number of foreign citizens visiting Kyrgyz Republic by main countries for 2000-11 (persons)**

	2000	2003	2005	2007	2008	2009	2010	2011
Total	**58 756**	**341 990**	**319 303**	**1 655 833**	**2 435 386**	**2 146 740**	**1 316 207**	**3 114 372**
Breakdown by country:								
Australia	171	616	732	1 292	1 504	1 883	1 189	1 375
Austria	214	350	439	675	765	1 046	536	510
Afghanistan	n.a.	235	384	634	525	461	404	493
Azerbijan	n.a.	400	492	1 566	1 237	1 158	984	3 983
Armenia	n.a.	213	266	580	508	407	293	982
Belarus	n.a.	336	394	1 192	938	937	517	1 685
Belgium	387	254	448	864	775	956	426	8
UK	1 426	2 743	2 974	4 519	3 261	3 827	2 716	1
Hungary	20	125	220	238	428	214	3 127	
Germany	1 811	8 553	9 128	9 794	10 010	9 374	6 980	8 432
Georgia	n.a.	342	345	729	698	549	610	898
Denmark	90	951	355	313	339	411	406	81
Israel	143	659	574	1 183	982	937	586	744
India	452	3 171	1 211	1 277	1 038	1 669	1 725	1 990
Iran	91	1 292	1 796	3 620	3 576	3 201	1 574	2 646
Spain	104	937	1798	2 130	1 580	1 152	459	38
Italy	334	704	946	1 044	1 112	1 278	902	1 427
Canada	636	1 077	1 296	1 632	1 597	1 859	1 669	1 904
China	1 074	8 268	15 747	20 201	21 921	21 879	18 167	25 059
Republic of Korea	342	2 700	3 850	6 417	4 526	4 790	4 207	3 378
Netherlands	449	1 647	1 029	787	684	788	385	20
Norway	89	676	355	422	380	523	371	232
Pakistan	53	697	2 973	1 731	1 699	1 952	2 082	2 044
Poland	199	351	393	861	1 014	786	524	713
Russia	n.a.	36 071	32 001	118 604	193 998	157 008	132 493	1 0201 02
Moldova	n.a.	n.a.	189	1 081	896	852	468	1 223
USA	3 979	11 667	11 727	13 775	7 983	9 464	7 473	12 878
Turkey	3 176	6 398	9 362	17 110	15 611	122 665	11 098	15 237
France	855	2 028	2 641	3 917	3 308	2 981	2 105	3 633
Finland	298	161	n.a.	240	245	291	230	510
Uzbekistan	n.a.	36 153	49 376	283 396	758 423	474 751	140 644	433 363
Tajikistan	n.a.	6 289	4 565	10 228	296 761	366 304	121 058	99 552

Notes: **n.a.**: data not available from the sources used.

The statistical data for Israel are supplied by and under the responsibility of the relevant Israeli authorities. The use of such data by the OECD is without prejudice to the status of the Golan Heights, East Jerusalem and Israeli settlements in the West Bank under the terms of international law.

Source: CIS Statistical Committee data for 2011, in SIAR (2013).

Table D.13. **Comparative analysis of average tourists' spending in 2006 and in 2012.**

Category of tourist	Tourist from non-CIS (in US dollars) | KGS)				Δ (%)		Kazakhstan (in US dollars) | KGS)				Δ (%)		Russia (in US dollars) | KGS)				Δ (%)		Domestic (in US dollars | KGS)				Δ (%)	
Year	2006		2012		Growth	Increase	2006		2012		Growth	Increase	2006		2012		Growth	Increase	2006		2012		Growth	Increase
Average daily spending	USD 49.1	KGS 2 263	USD 189.4	KGS 8 727	385.7	285.7	USD 43.5	KGS 2 005	USD 138.2	KGS 6 68	317.7	217.7	USD 52.2	KGS 2 405	USD 159.4	KGS 7 345	305.3	205.3	USD 18.4	KGS 848	USD 85.6	KGS 3 944	465.2	365.2

Source: Survey (100 individuals) conducted by SIAR (2013) in the Issyk-Kul region.

ORGANISATION FOR ECONOMIC CO-OPERATION AND DEVELOPMENT

The OECD is a unique forum where governments work together to address the economic, social and environmental challenges of globalisation. The OECD is also at the forefront of efforts to understand and to help governments respond to new developments and concerns, such as corporate governance, the information economy and the challenges of an ageing population. The Organisation provides a setting where governments can compare policy experiences, seek answers to common problems, identify good practice and work to co-ordinate domestic and international policies.

The OECD member countries are: Australia, Austria, Belgium, Canada, Chile, the Czech Republic, Denmark, Estonia, Finland, France, Germany, Greece, Hungary, Iceland, Ireland, Israel, Italy, Japan, Korea, Latvia, Luxembourg, Mexico, the Netherlands, New Zealand, Norway, Poland, Portugal, the Slovak Republic, Slovenia, Spain, Sweden, Switzerland, Turkey, the United Kingdom and the United States. The European Union takes part in the work of the OECD.

OECD Publishing disseminates widely the results of the Organisation's statistics gathering and research on economic, social and environmental issues, as well as the conventions, guidelines and standards agreed by its members.

OECD PUBLISHING, 2, rue André-Pascal, 75775 PARIS CEDEX 16
(97 2015 36 1 P) ISBN 978-92-64-24935-6 – 2016

www.ingramcontent.com/pod-product-compliance
Ingram Content Group UK Ltd.
Pitfield, Milton Keynes, MK11 3LW, UK
UKHW051241300926
15471UKWH00015B/1450

9 789264 249356